Boundaries For Dating After Divorce

Learn Smart Strategies to Make a Triumphant Return and Find Love In Your Relationship.

Wildine Pierre

© Copyright 2022 - All rights reserved.

The content contained within this book may not be reproduced, duplicated or transmitted without direct written permission from the author or the publisher.

Under no circumstances will any blame or legal responsibility be held against the publisher, or author, for any damages, reparation, or monetary loss due to the information contained within this book, either directly or indirectly.

Legal Notice

This book is copyright protected. It is only for personal use. You cannot amend, distribute, sell, use, quote or paraphrase any part, or the content within this book, without the consent of the author or publisher.

Disclaimer Notice

Please note the information contained within this document is for educational and entertainment purposes only. All effort has been executed to present accurate, up to date, reliable, complete information. No warranties of any kind are declared or implied. Readers acknowledge that the author is not engaged in the rendering of legal, financial, medical or professional advice. The content within this book has been derived from various sources. Please consult a licensed professional before attempting any techniques outlined in this book.

By reading this document, the reader agrees that under no circumstances is the author responsible for any losses, direct or indirect, that are incurred as a result of the use of the information contained within this document, including, but not limited to, errors, omissions, or inaccuracies.

Dedication

To the fierce queens strong enough to keep searching for love
Knowing that that a life without it, is like a sunless garden with dead flowers

Leave a Review

As an incentive for leaving a review, visit my website @ www.wildinepierre.com and sign up to be part of my fan club.

On the site you will find:

- Exclusive Q&A's with the author
- The books official page
- Several Giveaways and free flipbooks
- Chance to win an AUTOGRAPHED+ PERSONALIZED paperback of my latest release

And follow me on:

Facebook:https://www.facebook.com/wild.numa

Twitter:https://twitter.com/WildLovesWords

Instagram:https://www.instagram.com/p/Cf4ZWw_pPSH/?igshid=YmMyMTA2M2Y=

You're the best!!

–Wildine

Table Of Contents

Introduction 11

Chapter 1: Establishing Boundaries 16
   The Importance of Boundaries 17

Chapter 2: Stop Feeling Guilty 26
   Legitimate Reasons To Feel Guilty..28
   Difficulties In Accepting Guilt 30

Chapter 3: Choose Patience..39
   Take Time To Rediscover Your Best Self.................................. 41
   How Settled Are You About Your Divorce?................. 43
   Are You Clear About What You're Looking For? 44

Chapter 4: Learning To Love Yourself 47
   What Is This Experience Teaching You? 49
   5 Tips For Rediscovering Yourself 50

Chapter 5: Building Trust 57
   Take It Slow...58
   Learning To Re-Trust Someone 61
   6 Tips to Build Trust Again 63

Chapter 6: Be Kind To your Mind 66
   The Yin Yang Philosophy 68

Chapter 7: Recognizing The Red Flags 77

What Is A Dating Red Flag? 78

General Dating Red Flags 81

Red Flags When Dating in Your 50s (60s and 70s) 93

Red Flags In Dating A Divorced Man 95

Dating A Widower Red Flags 98

Dating A Narcissist Red Flags 101

Chapter 8: Recognizing Dangerous Intimacy 105

Intimacy Exists Outside Of Just Sex 107

Experiential Intimacy 115

Spiritual Intimacy 117

What To Do About The Fear Of Intimacy 124

Chapter 9: Effective Communication 128

Communication Builds Both Parties In A Relationship 129

Communication Helps You Grow Together 130

Is There Such A Thing As Over-Communication? 131

How To Communicate 132

Chapter 10: State Your Needs And Intentions 146

How Do You Know Your Intentions? 147

What Do Intentions Mean? 148

What Are Good Intentions? 149

10 Tips On How To Set Intentions 150

Chapter 11: Social Media Boundaries 156

The Dangers Of Social Media When It Comes To Relationships 156

How To Navigate Social Media Boundaries 162

Give Your Partner The Benefit Of The Doubt 168

Chapter 12: Establish Mutual Communication 169

    Defining Emotional Connection 169

    Signs of Emotional Connection 171

Chapter 13: Set Healthy Limits 177

    Six Tips For Setting Healthy Boundaries 178

    Boundaries To Protect 180

    Protecting Yourself Financially 183

Chapter 14: Keep Your Dignity Intact 187

    Maintain Mutual Respect 188

    Do Not Compromise On Dignity 188

    Live With Dignity 189

    Love Has A Limit, And Its Name Is Dignity 190

    The Pride And Dignity Of Self-Love 191

    Dignity Has A Very High Price 192

    How To Gain More Power 193

Chapter 15: Build A Solid Foundation 197

    How To Start Building Or Reinforcing That Foundation 198

Chapter 16: Co-Parenting Boundaries 202

    What Is Co-Parenting? 202

    The Three Relationships 203

    Talk to Your Ex 204

    Talk to Your Children 205

    Be Honest With Your New Partner 207

    Ask About Your Partner's Wishes 208

    Boundaries With Discipline 208

    What Will You Share About Your Child? 209

    Keep Communicating With Each Other 210
Conclusion **211**
    Consider What You're Searching For 212
    Value Yourself 212
    Contemplate Counseling 212
    Be Honest 213
Also by the Author **214**
References **219**

Introduction

I admit dating is a tricky concept for most of us. After going through a divorce, it can feel even more slippery. My rule of thumb is always to allow yourself enough time to heal. You should be ready to try something new rather than force yourself.

In other words, don't focus on the length of time it takes for you to get to the "I'm ready to date" phase. Instead, focus on what you do in the meantime. Your energy should have a room of its own to nourish and replenish itself.

Love can become exhausting because you have constantly conformed to the drone of "give, give, give." All of us have experienced difficult breakups, but divorce is different. The pain of separation runs deep roots in the soil. You need to split all assets, and lives get uprooted. Divorces become messy and drawn out.

Significant life transitions take time to get used to, and a divorce is no different. When separating from the person you've been closest to, it doesn't matter how long you've been married. Indeed, you went through the motions making sure it was the right move, asking yourself all the necessary questions in advance, and talking to your children thoroughly. But now, the decisions have been made.

Boundaries are essential to ensure everyone in your family can transition to the idea of you finding a healthy relationship. Your children will have views and beliefs of their own. A few children may respond positively to a new adult figure playing a role in their lives. However, others may not be ready to see their parents with an apparent stranger. The resultant fears and anxiety may lead to their thinking you aren't paying them as much attention as you usually would.

As a newly single parent, the idea of dating can feel like an added burden to the already existing pile of household chores. Some of you might even be eager to meet new people once the emotional cyclone of recovering from a divorce has died. But, pause and consider what I am about to say carefully.

The whole world of external love is waiting, but for a little while, let all of it come from within your soul. Reflecting on everything that has been part of your life's story will help you grieve for what is lost while also preparing you to look forward to new chapters. You learn to instinctively understand how to meander through a relationship and love "better" instead of "harder." Once you feel ready, this book is here to make things simpler.

So, if you have gone through the earlier paragraphs and are still here, I assume you feel ready. In this case, welcome to the start of what will be a new start.

Going through a divorce is one of the most challenging pathways you could ever have to walk. Years back, when I witnessed what it does to a family in real life, I understood that no amount of love could prepare you for the feeling of insecurity and hopelessness. So, let me begin this journey with a small affirmation. You are unique, strong, and brave.

Divorce is overwhelming. Life itself becomes monochromatic for a period. You wonder where you went wrong. How did the one relationship that was supposed to sustain you till the end break you into tiny little shards?

Part of the confusion immediately resulting after you separate from your long-term partner results from the sudden removal of codependency. You feel vulnerable and fragile. Your boundaries are all over the place now, and it can seem like a mammoth task to get everything in order.

Dear reader, I know what it feels like to have to walk through this fire. The mere thought of another relationship—doing everything all over again— can be the most harrowing thing on your mind. Forget falling in love; you may not even be ready to step out of the house and partake in social life! Plus, how do you ensure the following liaisons don't destroy you the same way? How do you know you will not make the same mistakes or fall into the same traps?

I read something beautiful some months back from a page called *The Artidote*— you may have heard of it too. The contributor made a pretty little artwork with the caption, *"I noticed the patterns, so I made a choice."* The picture was of an almost complete cycle breaking at the end, with a line entering below into another trajectory. The new pattern lies in setting up frontiers that will not leave you with regrets or the depressing feeling of a loved one using you.

The thing is— dating is beautiful and done right; it can be one of the best things in your life after an exhausting divorce. The prospects and possibilities are endless! The world is once again your oyster, and you have the freedom to choose someone in your new, mature, and more grounded state of being. Young love can often be explosive, but now? Now you are readying yourself to do *what is best for your soul.*

If you feel ready and the heavy emotions burdening your mind and body following divorce have lightened, let's take the next step. You may be at a loss when it comes to dating. A multitude of questions may be running through your mind. "What if I choose the wrong person?" "What if my kid(s) hate them?" "What if history repeats itself?"

Well, to that, I will just quote some of my favorite lines ever to have existed. When Erin Hanson wrote these lines, she made something that resonated with my soul. I think you will learn, in time, to feel the same way.

"What if I fall?
But oh, my darling,
What if you fly?"

The world is a beautiful and terrifying place. But what is life if you don't experience everything that makes living worth the time given to you? So, let us discover how you can make the next episode of your life the most beautiful and adventurous one yet.

Chapter 1
Establishing Boundaries

Imagine this. You finally feel as if things are settling down. Your child(ren) is getting used to the presence of a single parent around them. They even give you more of their time. You begin to believe everything will be alright.

Then, one day out of the blue, your child tells you they want to spend more time with your ex-partner. I know how hurtful this can seem, but again, this is one of the many reasons boundaries are so important. Just like you need space to recover, they need to be around both parents to make sense of what has happened.

Establishing boundaries in the wake of a divorce is necessary, not just for your personal space but also for your children, extended family, former in-laws, not to mention your parenting partner.

Boundaries will keep your family unit functional while reducing the stress of dealing with all the changes. They will allow you to work together as a unit, maintaining everyone's sanity as intact as possible. Plus, they give you the chance to sort things amicably.

You will see an apparent physical and emotional detachment settling in place once you begin setting boundaries. Within this space, it will be possible for you to invest time in self-care and self-expression.

The focus you need on other essential things, like devoting your time to your children, family, profession, and future, will become more oriented. At the same time, you can work on fostering mutual respect with your ex-partner.

The Importance of Boundaries

Consider this. You are driving down a two-lane road. You see a car coming from the opposite direction. An inner impulse may urge you not to obey the law and move to the left of the centerline. But if you do so, it will be an offense, and you could also risk immense danger to the other car's driver and yourself.

Boundaries exist for a reason, and the simple thing is, if they weren't there, your life would be an endless tirade of you doing things that hurt you and those around you. They help you stay in your lane while ensuring others feel content.

Let's say you love pets, and your home is full of them. As a homeowner, you may have a fence dividing your property from your neighbor's. The fence serves to remind your families where different properties begin and end. They keep things from going out of hand. For instance, without a fence, a pet might cross the boundary of your home, enter your neighbor's, and do something that earns their wrath.

One of the unfortunate things about this world is that not everyone feels the same way regarding who and what we love. I know we adore our pets with our whole hearts and souls, but you will often find people around you don't feel the same way. Boundaries remind you that as a homeowner and a responsible pet parent, you must do what is necessary to protect your pet from harm at the hands of potential strangers.

In the same way, the presence of cubicle walls or some other form of delimitation separates your workspace from your colleagues at work. Imagine if that wasn't there. Everyone would be able to see what you were doing *all the time!* You need the peace of that tiny cubicle to be able to do your thing without the constant worry of multiple eyes on you.

Of course, there are times in the day when the boundaries extend. For instance, when you are sharing lunch with other colleagues. For this purpose, it is essential to know that your limits are always subjective, making them beautiful.

Your neighbor may love your pet and be happy to have them over. Your workspace may be full of supportive colleagues who love to share and work. In such cases, your boundaries can be far more fluid. Nonetheless, they need to be there to remind you *are your own person,* existing separate from and in harmony with the world.

Relationships Need Boundaries

Boundaries are inherent in all healthy partnerships. Here's an example of how it works visually: Imagine you and your partner are facing each other. A defined line on the ground separates you that extends to the left and right as far as you can see in either direction.

Let me explain a little further. Every item on your side belongs to you; every article on the other side of the line belongs to your partner. This is not to say you cannot share your lives. It is only a reminder to both of you to retain your individual identities while operating as a team.

You love your partner with your entire heart. You also trust them with every detail of your life. For the whole duration of your relationship, they are the ones controlling and micromanaging your finances. When it comes to finances, you decide you don't want to be bothered to handle your accounts, so you let them do this for the both of you.

Then one day, you are no longer partners. After years of not knowing the alphabet of how your finances work, how to do your taxes, or even gauge your savings, will you be able to hold your own?

It is possible, but it will take a mammoth effort. For this and so many other tiny reasons, maintaining control over the things about your identity while sharing yourself with your partner is the definition of a wholesome relationship founded on boundaries.

Boundaries Define Ownership And Responsibility.

In romantic partnerships, partners cannot always define the "things" they share as material. So, you may be unable to use a fence or a cubicle to delineate boundaries between your partner and you. In this case, the boundary line will exist to define how much you will do for your partner and vice versa.

In other words, these are natural and intangible limits to help you stay sane. These limits will benefit every relationship when partners understand, respect, and agree to abide by them.

Another way of saying this: boundaries distinguish your responsibility in the relationship from that of your partner. What is each person in the relationship responsible for? Think for a second. When it comes to your identity, what would you say constitutes your core self? Our entities have six independent constructs.

- Bodies
- Words
- Emotions
- Attitudes
- Values
- Preferences

So, if you don't want to be touched on occasion because you are tired, or it feels out of place, or simply because you aren't in the mood, you have the right to say no. Suppose you say unkind words to your partner, you take responsibility for those words and apologize.

If your partner asks you why you are quiet, you have a commitment to try and help them understand what you are feeling instead of letting them guess. But, in the same breath, if speaking or communicating feels like you are interacting with a living, breathing wall, you have the right to say, "I have done all I could. If you still cannot understand why I am upset, this is where I draw the line."

Boundaries Eliminate Blame

My mother used to tell me something beautiful. Whenever I got too angry, she would sit me down, look into my eyes, and say these words. *"When you get too angry, you can't see yourself. And, if you can't see yourself clearly, you will never be able to set or maintain healthy boundaries."*

What do we understand when associating "healthy" with boundaries? Here are the four-fold truths I inherently believe. A healthy limit will—Allow mature communications to thrive, even during disagreements.

- Let me have my share myself without fostering needy codependency.

- Give me my personal space.

- Create room for voicing concerns over holding onto resentment or hate.

Blame is almost always a maneuver to deflect ownership off a problem. When you have space for flourishing discussions, the tendency to blame your partner for every little mistake gets significantly reduced. Boundaries help you to see your contribution to a misunderstanding or conflict.

Having well-defined boundaries, therefore, aids in establishing where one begins and ends. They also help you and your spouse define your respective roles in a relationship.

It takes a lot of courage to be able to look inwards and take responsibility for your share of mishaps. We usually blame the other person without clear sight because that is so much easier. But, with a boundary in place, you will intrinsically want to be accountable for what is yours.

Emotional closeness has a solid foundation to expand on when responsibility lines are defined and respected by all parties. But if they aren't respected or recognized, problems develop because you are always looking to shift blame.

In most cases, relationships built on love have an element of possessiveness attached, meaning disagreements will flare from time to time. Perhaps there was hurt on both sides. But suppose you have your boundaries in place.

In that case, you automatically know, "I will try to sort this out maturely before exploding." Since both of you take responsibility for your mistakes, the problem gets solved much quicker.

Common Boundary Violations

Respect is key to getting anything to work. When your partner oversteps the limits you have set for your relationship, it can get destructive, even if it's accidental. You may feel you cannot say how hurt you are, which causes emotions to get bottled up. The damage deepens into anger and resentment.

Emotional distance grows between the two of you. Your partner feels they can't do anything without earning your wrath. You think it's a waste of time trying to reason with them. The result is an unsatisfying relationship that has all but broken down.

Let's take a look at some behaviors signaling boundary issues in romantic partnerships—

You say "yes" too often to your partner even if your heart's not in the act. Maybe they want to be intimate, but you aren't in the mood. Perhaps they want to go out with their friends, but you'd like it if they spent the night with you.

Or, it could be that they had promised to go on a trip with you but asked if it's okay to cancel at the last minute. On all these occasions, you go along with their desires because you want to please them or avoid any form of confrontation. On the other hand, you could also be refusing a request because you want to punish them.

Let's say they come home late after a long day at work. You have prepared a special dinner for them, and you feel angry.

When they ask you, "can we please talk about it?" your anger gets in the way. You forget the boundary you set for yourself—to respect your commitment to them. So, you end up saying, "no, I'm not in the mood." They are left to do pages of guesswork on where they went wrong.

In both of the above instances, you are not respecting the notions of an honest or wholesome relationship. You need to reexamine your boundaries regarding how much you want to give to them and how true you are to yourself and your relationship.

Tips To Establish And Maintain Healthy Boundaries

Anything worth saving takes time and effort. Cultivate genuine, respectful conversations which will allow mutual sharing of feelings and thoughts between you. At all points, communicate how you think and feel with honesty and clarity.

Of course, there will be occasions where immediate solutions are next to impossible. It's fine to ask for time to sort things out, so long as you actually "ask" instead of avoiding all means of communication. Don't shirk your partner, and don't walk away from future discussions.

Ask your partner how they are feeling rather than making assumptions at random. Each of you has thoughts and feelings, and you are responsible for putting them into words the other may understand. This way, your partner doesn't have to guess what you think at each point. Trust me; it gets exhausting wondering, "are they mad at me," every minute of every day. Don't do that to someone so close to you.

Accept responsibility for the decisions you make. Ask yourself how your intended or accidental choices may have contributed to the situation rather than blaming your partner for your feelings or what is happening. As I mentioned, we run to berate ourselves or destroy those who want the best for us when things go out of whack. To prevent that, pause for a minute and count to ten whenever something goes wrong.

Take deep, relaxing breaths, and ask yourself: "is this a battle I choose?" Let me tell you— not all battles are worth fighting, and in a partnership, there will always be those instances when fights are just going to happen. Save your precious breath for those. Don't flare up at every tiny issue that shows up, and take a breather just to think, "Is this worth hurting them? Will I not regret it later?"

Express the sentiments that are uniquely yours without pointing the finger at your partner. For example, it is far more effective to say, "I feel wounded and misunderstood in this conversation" than to say to someone, "You made me feel upset because of how you spoke to me." With the former, you are merely expressing an emotion. In the latter instance, however, you are saying something deliberately hurtful and targeting your partner as the reason behind how you feel.

Establishing healthy limits takes time and effort, especially if you come from a family where boundaries were not clearly defined or were seldom acknowledged. You and your partner will better determine where the boundary line should be in your relationship as you both gain more experience. As a consequence of this, your connection will become more resilient with time.

Chapter 2
Stop Feeling Guilty

The motions involved in a divorce are distressing enough. You are preparing to uproot the most profound sense of familiarity— the aspect of your life you thought was a given until your last breath. Added to that is something I like to call "separation guilt."

The cycle of grief following every divorce is pretty much a guarantee. So, you acquire one, and the other follows. It happens just like the sun rises and sets, and you can't avoid it.

Ironically, the earth has places where you could escape sunlight for months. But, even if you divorce in these places, you'd still face divorce guilt. The very burden of adding the mess of "I feel so terrible/ what have I done/ this is all my fault" to the pile of stale feelings may feel highly unfair.

My first advice is, don't think you are alone in this. There's a good chance your partner is bearing the same guilt as you. If not, millions of others go through the same process, which is a legitimate step in healing.

Guilt usually follows after we perceive we have done something terrible or ethically corrupt. It's the natural effect of having a conscience. Whenever you act in ways that don't quite meet the boundaries set by your moral compass, you experience guilt.

We may not quite understand this, but sometimes, guilt can be highly multi-faceted. There are some situations where we should take the onus of the choices we make on our shoulders. On other occasions, guilt may simply result from a complicated cocktail of emotions, *even if we haven't really done anything wrong.*

The problem with divorce guilt is that it can exist even for those amongst us who decide to separate for all the right reasons. You may feel slightly defensive at this stage, which is wholly justified. It's exhausting to constantly defend your actions and choices to others, much less yourself.

A while back, I discovered that despite our best efforts, we often feel guilty about things over which we have no control by surveying divorced men and women. This was a troubled time in my own life— ironically enough, while listening to others' stories, I suddenly realized that I had missed the warning indications of my own relationship's demise. Looking back, I now realize this was a crucial phase I had to go through to understand myself and my family better.

Legitimate Reasons To Feel Guilty

Four predominant themes stand out to me when I consider the concept of divorce guilt.

One, there is the guilt because you've messed up. Two, you feel guilty about something you *think* you've done. Three, guilt arises from believing you didn't help someone as much as they needed you to. Four, there is self-condemnation: *how could I possibly be doing better than them?*

The thing is, when someone is filing for a divorce, there is an implicit or explicit understanding and acknowledgment that too much water has flown between the two people who make up the relationship. A long damage period has existed that either a single partner or both want to let go of. People feel guilty for the tiniest of things.

We have guilt for leaving. Guilt for staying. So, we could sit and ruminate for hours as to the "why" or "who" or "how" of it all. We could think that culpability rests on us for filing or because we refused to change "the way they wanted us to."

However, none of it will alter where we are right now, and the only way out of this rabbit hole is to acknowledge that it's okay to hurt. In itself, guilt symbolizes the negative feelings arising from a wrong behavior or a perception of the same.

Under many circumstances, guilt is useful. It keeps our moral selves in check and stops us from acting out in ways that may be dangerous. In intimate relationships, however, it's a different ballgame. It makes us witness the negative impact of our supposed behaviors on those we love the most. And that's not easy.

Of course, there are legitimate potholes from which divorce guilt can unfurl. These include, but aren't limited to:

Badmouthing your ex-partner in a bout of anger or being rude to them before your children.

- Unintentionally making things difficult for your ex-partner in terms of spending time with your children or sharing resources like assets and money.

- Bringing strangers home on multiple occasions when the children are around.

- Engaging in an illicit romance.

- A repeated return to a destructive addiction.

- Some form of abuse, whether intended or otherwise.

- Debt arising from overspending or not contributing to the house and the family as much as your ex-partner.

- Shifting blame one too many times,

- Failing or lack of sexual intimacy, and

- Just wanting to leave because "you want to live your own life."

So, if one of these points fits you, begin by taking a deep breath. Dear reader, it will be okay. I know that seems furthest from how you feel right now, but I promise there is a silver lining. And this lies in learning to forgive others, but most of all—yourself.

Difficulties In Accepting Guilt

The implication of "being" guilty is that you've done something wrong. So, don't let it make you more miserable than you already are or trap you in a prison of opinions and judgment. But in making this ultimate choice (that is, divorcing), you are doing something helpful to yourself.

You aren't a jerk for choosing to put your happiness first. Sadness, anger, and all those feelings are normal and healthy breakup fodder. But guilt can be a problem when it prevents you from making a good decision. If legitimate reasons were driving the divorce wheel, try not to let feelings of remorse get in the way of you doing what is right.

If you made mistakes during your alliance, consider altering the hurtful behavior patterns before it is too late because holding on to the guilt and the regret that stems from it won't help in the long run. To rise above your guilt, you need to know it is an *unavoidable* emotion.

Understand: all of us commit mistakes that weigh heavy on the conscience. As long as you are willing to address the issues arising, you will be alright— as will your ex-partner and the family.

The things we cannot run away from the need to be faced head-on. The key is to learn from mistakes, take responsibility for your actions, and restore faith in your ability to move forward. Find solutions that will allow you to forgive yourself and give you the strength to move forward. If it feels too tricky alone, take the help of a therapist.

Now, let me share some experiences I have acquired over the years. Handling life after divorce was difficult, and I instinctively veered toward people who had encountered similar experiences. What began as an effort to understand and navigate the pain culminated in my meeting wonderful people who had decided to divorce because it was *necessary*.

Infidelity. Failure to pay attention to the children. Abuse. You name it. I saw it all. Yet, the most beautiful of the people I met felt guilty, even after enduring so much neglect— for so many years. I could not help empathizing, and in the process, I learned immensely about the entire concept of divorce guilt. These people— now my friends and close associations— helped me realize that everything else in the world is secondary to your perception of yourself.

When you are alone in a room at night, with nothing but your thoughts for company, you should be able to look inward and think, "I had to make some difficult decisions, but they amounted to the right things."

In the first instance, my overall surprise stemmed from how suddenly divorce seems to make a guest appearance— entirely unexpected— with model families. A woman who initiated divorce after a 25+ year marriage says, "I feel guilty because I was so good at sweeping things under the rug to keep the peace. My kids were shocked.

Naturally, they had no idea I was unhappy. I did them a disservice by not having more boundaries and speaking up. My children how feel their lives have been riddled with lies and half-truths." When she left the marriage, her adult children were angry with her.

In another instance, a man reported, "I want to individual counseling to figure out whether I wanted to stay married. It was hard. My ex and children didn't want me to leave. Part of the guilt that I felt six months into the separation was for not doing more before the split."

Most splits have an element where one partner feels guilty for doing the bulk of the "deserting." You have to know that when a divorce is finalized, it's because someone has given up hope for the marriage. And it is likely they feel guilty about pulling the plug and the impact of doing this on those they care about.

Another person reported: "I felt guilty because I couldn't make him happy in 15 years." This is another recurring theme when people condemn themselves for the marriage going south. It is also an instance where we feel guilty for things we shouldn't.

The woman who said these words was married to an angry, selfish narcissist who took advantage of her guilt for the decade and five years they were together. When they separated, he left with the bulk of their financial assets.

My question is: what did the husband do to "fix" things, other than go with most of their coupled resources? Yet, even after such serious efforts, she still felt guilty.

All of the people I spoke of are the ones who have tried all they could to save their family and marriage from going to the dust. And boy, did they give it their all. Here are some of the things they did:

- Reading countless books – especially Jennifer Weiner and The Divorce Remedy, among many others,

- Trying Counseling – couples and individuals – probably at least six different times during the marriage,

- Participating in Save Your Marriage weekend,

Going for initiated dates,

- Spending time together without the kids,

- Starting a business venture to spend more time with each other,

- Supporting the ex-partner's hobbies,

- Talking with other couples that stayed together after betrayals/challenges,

- Having the ex-partner's parents talk with them,

- Having their parents talk with them,

- Talking with their friends about strategies to improve the marriage,

- Ignoring their own needs for intimacy to accommodate their challenging circumstances, and even

- Writing letters to their ex-partner.

Ultimately, the only place it landed them was in the courtroom, trying to make peace with the separation. When the differences are irreconcilable, there's only so much you can do before knowing the only way to peace lies through walking two different routes.

A common theme through divorce guilt is choosing personal happiness over others, in many cases for the first time. So, when someone says, "I made my needs secondary throughout my marriage," it isn't surprising to find the fragile bonds weakening into nothing over time.

Divorce becomes the last option— but the mind, forever stuck in the rut of habit, keeps throwing the onus on the unfortunate souls who feel their happiness is "not as important." They feel guilty being happier or relieved after the divorced.

I've also known people to feel guilty about enjoying time away from their children. We know our decision to end the marriage will impact our children. Often, it throws them into a period of depression, feeling uncertain about their future with each of their parents and what the family will look like. When married, we don't need to attend every child's activities because our partners pick up the slack. But when we divorce, we feel guilty about missing these.

We may feel bad about our child's sufferings— so much so that saying no to their requests becomes impossible. Added to that is the hotpot of their childlike version of events, molded by the people they "thought" their parents were. They may not have even known the inner cracks, so they ask innocent (but hurtful) questions like, *"Were we the family I thought we were? I never saw my parents fighting; was it that bad? If my mom/dad is such a bad person to be married to, why don't they look unhappy?"*

Here's what one of my associates told me about her divorce:

"I covered up a lot of what was wrong with our family life before divorcing. I took on more than my fair share of the parenting tasks, leaving my ex to focus on work and his interests. I walked on eggshells over sensitive topics because I wanted to avoid cause conflict. I shielded the kids from all our troubles. They had no idea anything was wrong.

We didn't fight much, and if we did, it was late at night, behind closed doors. I did what I thought was right, but it didn't give my kids a very accurate picture of married life or coping with lousy behavior. So much of my guilt about my divorce was wondering if I had done enough and if I had harmed my kids by the way I handled things while I was married."

Many of us think that divorcing is a sure-shot way to disappoint our families and faith, much less ourselves. Over time, the red signals we ignored become waving flags, and we feel guilty that we stayed too long to try to make it work.

Then there's the remorse of never being enough for the person we loved so dearly once upon a time. We also feel terrible about being excited about the possibility of finding new love. Come to think of it; there are so many reasons for divorce guilt it seems impossible to list them all.

What Can We Do About This Guilt?

Divorce guilt is not for the faint of heart. Only warriors know how hard it is to feel hunted by your thoughts constantly. It will pursue you in the death of night, jab spears at your heart during business hours, and leave you bleeding and limp at the feet of the people you want desperately to protect. It's ruthless.

With possibilities for feelings of guilt nearly endless with divorce, the key is forgiving yourself and moving forward so you can build a new life. The first step lies in realizing you can't get around it except by *going through it.*

- Process your guilt by feeling it. Write about it, talk to friends or a therapist, and accept that it is a temporary stage.

- Have compassion for the people who are hurting due to your choices but do not falter from your decisions.

This isn't a game you can save and return to each time something goes wrong. It's a choice you have made for your sanity and health of the mind. Be true to yourself.

- Keep your kids and their best interests at the heart of your decision-making and shield them as much as you can. Don't discuss topics that will upset them unless they approach you, looking for answers. When you speak to them about deep issues, treat them with compassion and respect, and let them know that both of you will always love and be there to guide them. During visitations, if your ex is a trigger for you, arrange for a neutral drop-off and minimize your interaction.

- Get healthy and make self-care a priority. Find yourself a therapist, take a divorce class, seek out a coach, trainer, gym membership, and whatever else you need to orient your life in the right direction. It has taken a lot of courage to get yourself to this position; now, make the most of it.

- Don't shirk off the heavier details. They will keep piling up until they become too messy to cope with. Call a lawyer or mediator, divide assets, file the divorce papers, and move forward.

At the heart of it, try to keep things as amicable as possible without falling into stagnation. I know it feels like "tomorrow" will be the better day to sign those papers or tell the kids, but when tomorrow comes, it will feel just as gray. The longer the relationship is in limbo, the harder it is for everyone to transition.

Letting go isn't about forgetting, but about learning and moving on. It's choosing to be strengthened by your past, not strangled by it.

Though guilt may be inevitable, it doesn't have to be endless. Do yourself (and those who love you) a favor and release it, a little bit at a time. You did the best you knew how to do at the time. Take your mistakes with a grain of salt, and let them define your future decisions rather than limit all your present actions.

When you think of healing, you always want to begin by looking inwards first. Take care of yourself. The world looks up to people who don't sell themselves short.

Chapter 3
Choose Patience

When I was a young girl, my mother liked to tell me something time and again. She knew that I would grow up, fall in love, and, if fate was kind enough, have it uplift and free me. But, she was also practical enough to understand chances of that happening in a world that grows increasingly selfish were dim. So, she told me to take my time to heal. Learning inner peace, one tiny step at a time— isn't that what makes life so beautiful?

When we jump into relationships, one after the other, without taking time to acknowledge the hurt and grief inside us, we often injure the new people we date. After my first relationship hit the rocks, so to speak, I rushed into another just a few months later. I shirked off my mother's worries and told her, "I'm just having fun— exploring the waters." Until another heartbreak followed, and then another.

Do not drag anybody else into your mess and drama if you are going through a separation, and do not start dating a few days into a painful divorce. You are now on a roller coaster ride that will do everyone you bring along with you. I don't just mean people external to you.

> Your own inner soul is in turmoil. Your assets need dividing.

> Your home is changing.

These are big things to deal with and weigh heavy on the heart. Covering a thick rug over them in the form of an exciting stranger may seem easy, but easy doesn't make it worthwhile or even useful in the long run. What will it do if you wake up a few months from now with a person you cannot relate to or someone who does not understand your pain-- simply because you chose to rush? Therefore, wait.

It took me years to realize the pattern I had gotten caught up in so subconsciously. But once I did, I chose to break away. We often get swept away when we seek out quick attractions. The new people may be attracted to us by our seeming vulnerabilities. They may want to "protect" us from the vagaries of the world. They may even tell us, "I'm not going to hurt you as they did."

I can give you one honest word of advice— *hurt you, they will.* A time will come when these seemingly incredible and *"they-can-do-no-wrong"* entities will grow tired of your inner demons— those you refused to handle and kept pushing under the rug. And when that happens, it will inevitably result in another heartbreak. So, to find love, *you, need to begin by giving it to yourself first.*

The notion of time, however, is subjective to where you're at in the healing process. Finding a new relationship quickly after separation may be more manageable if you genuinely feel ready. For others, it may take a long while before feeling emotions that strong again. Don't doubt the potential of a slow burn. And most of all, don't push yourself to date because "there are only so many fishes left in the pool." It isn't a competition— especially not when you are on the verge of self-discovery.

Don't feel discouraged if it takes a good handful of dates to start feeling a spark and attraction toward a new romantic interest in your life. Lust and passion can feel intoxicating, but real connections take time and respect. So, if it feels like you're ready to swim but not dive, let your potential partners know you aren't looking for a monogamous relationship. And truly mean it— be sure to have talked with yourself.

You can't think, "I want to have fun, but maybe I can also get serious with them." That's a dangerous bet, especially if both parties only take things "lightly." So, be mindful with every step you take, and at all points, choose patience. The key lies in feeling good about what you are doing.

Take Time To Rediscover Your Best Self

The singles scene is teeming with people, most mentally unprepared to deal with the emotional nuances of relationships following a divorce. On the first date, they'll likely be the ones going into tedious detailing of their "horrible" ex. They can also repeatedly seek validation that they are deserving of love and physically desirable. You may feel worried about missed chances, but trust me, external love can wait.

There's nothing wrong with exploring this scene and finding someone who could potentially become the yin to your yang. But think about this realistically. Are you ready to parent another grown-up, especially when trying to mend yourself? I'd say it's an additional burden you don't need. Wait until you feel ready. It's okay to focus on yourself and enjoy being alone before going through the motions of finding that "special somebody."

In the meantime, improve your spiritual and physical well-being. Take time to do the self-care things you always pushed for "when the kids aren't home" or "when I have a little me-time." *This* is your me-time. Don't forget to do a little dreaming as well. Set visions for what you'd like your life to encapsulate three, six, or twelve months from today. Begin goal-setting, and enlist small steps propelling you closer and closer to the big aspirations.

Dedicating energy inward and focusing on becoming your best self will reward you much more than lackluster dates spent mothering other people. You will find more peace and have new and stronger faith in your capabilities. A side note— I can tell you there's nothing quite as sexy and attractive as a person who can own themselves. Not only are they pleasant to be around, but their energy also attracts positivity and joy.

The world loves warriors who know which battles to pick and choose. When you seek to become a well-rounded human being, you put out a resonant frequency into the world, and people are drawn to you because of the sun in your spirit and the kindness in your soul.

The gift you're giving yourself right now— this lesson that involves you rising to your best and most wholesome self, will go further than restoring your confidence, peace, and clarity of mind. You will also discover the purpose of external relationships doesn't lie in completing you but rather in enriching and adding to what you already have and *who you already are.* When you realize this, you'll know you're ready.

As you go deeper into rediscovering yourself, you'll be surprised at how resilient you become. You'll form an innate understanding of what you need, the things which don't merit your time or tolerance, and the essentials that should define your subsequent relationships. Taken together, this will make dating after divorce simpler, easier, and so much more fun!

How Settled Are You About Your Divorce?

I always say an essential step in recovery is to persist through the tide of emotions until a day comes when you wake up thinking, "wow, I don't feel the way I used to." And trust me, this isn't easy. It is, however, imperative to be past the stage where you experience emotional extremes whenever you think of your ex.

The mere smell of a familiar shampoo or aftershave, looking at a dish they liked to eat, or chancing upon a song both of you loved should not reduce you to a weeping sponge. You need to wait until the day you can hear a piece of music or visit a place that holds memories of both of you and only remember things fondly, without any hate, anger, or regret. And for a while, negative emotions will exist— until they don't.

Another very pertinent concern is— is there any part of you that hopes to reconcile with the ex? Dating is meant to work its charm if you are genuinely comfortable in the reality of your marriage ending. If you aren't at this stage yet, that's fine. If there is an infinitesimally slight chance, don't take on the risk of dating.

I've been part of those situations where people feel, "we need to explore the waters and see if we can find ourselves back to each other." Trust me, more often than not, you end up hurting others in the process, and if you perchance see your ex moving on with someone who makes them happy (while you still hope they find their way back to you), hell breaks loose.

Are You Clear About What You're Looking For?

A lot of things will be different once you're ready. You are now more mature than when you first fell in love, so your expectations from a potential partner will also change.

To make the process painless, build a solid idea about what you want in the people you meet. You should have absolute security in knowing:

- Dealbreakers and red flags,

- Qualities that matter,

- Communication styles and methods that comfort you and those that don't,

- The question of children (if relevant),

- An upgraded version of what was your "type" factoring in your stage in life,

- Whether you want something serious or are content to explore, and

- Whether exclusivity is a no-brainer for you.

As a newly single individual, you have earned the freedom to meet exciting people. But they'd be just as exciting tomorrow and the day after. You could push self-healing to "the next day," or "Monday," or "next week," but every step you take in ignorance thrusts you down a rabbit hole of darkness and overdependence on the outer world. What's the rush? Give yourself room to appreciate the changes happening in your life before sharing the room with someone else.

Every relationship, including marriage, takes time to heal from once things go south. Who ended things is irrelevant here. There will always be residual feelings that'll need redressal. Additionally, marriage comes with a safety guarantee. You go into it expecting a shared life, and once it is no longer real, it's like being told the one thing you were sure of has let you down.

It'll be a while before you untangle all the knots and process the loss, and this untangling is no different from grieving after the passing of a loved one. In a sense, you are experiencing grief now, too— for the demise of a relationship. Don't put expectations or deadlines on the plan; instead, focus on healing regardless of the duration it takes. The world of new romance is waiting, and it will embrace you just as hard (perhaps more so) when you are ready to enjoy it fully.

Chapter 4
Learning To Love Yourself

The worst thing about a divorce isn't what it does. It's what it reduces you to. For a long time following a painful separation, you will feel inadequate and lesser than a whole person. This is likely due to sincerely giving too much of yourself to someone you loved. Empaths have a hard time with the world, primarily because of how willingly they give of themselves and how malicious circumstances can play out.

I know because I've been there, dear reader. I even recall a day when I sat, prettily decked up in a cozy restaurant, unable to answer a simple, "what do you like to do?" This was supposed to be easy, right? After all the hardships I had endured, how could such a characterless question push me to the verge of an emotional breakdown in a packed restaurant, so much so that I had to excuse myself and get out of there as quickly as I could? How could I not even know what I liked to do?

It turns out I was too busy being "their" people. My partner's wife. My children's mom. And there was nothing wrong with those roles— as a matter of fact, my role as a mom makes me more and more proud and fulfilled every day. The issue was that I allowed my external identities to become predominant and rule over all other aspects of my life, including my inner and infinitely precious self.

When we get married and eventually become parents, our sole focus alters to factor in our children and spouses. At times, this focus can become larger than life. We unconsciously allow them to take everything we have until a time comes when we are reduced to being identified only through titles like "wife," and indeed, it's a beautiful title. Still, it should not be synonymous with the entirety of our existence. The fact of being a "wife" should be something that adds to and enriches our identities as individual people without occupying all the space we have to offer.

The first step to recovering your mental health following a separation is acknowledging and forgiving yourself. Self-blame and frustration will be natural consequences of realizing we have allowed too many people to overstep their boundaries. We have been martyrs in our marriages for too long, but that does not mean we need to become hosts of parasitic anger over spilled milk.

Just like right now, the realization that we should have put ourselves first is hitting us organically. Rather than wallowing over wasted time, we could now choose to go the route of self-love. Every day spent in anger at all the "could haves" and "should haves" are days lost. It's up to us to choose how much time we want to spend prioritizing those we've had to let go. Even as we feel angry and remorseful, *we still prioritize them and how we think/used to feel when we married them.*

Once you are past this step, take a long, hard look into all the primary and secondary factors that constituted the entirety of your marriage. Consider what made you feel "used" or what instances compelled you to give in and surrender too extensively. Going through this will take weeks if you're already past the "this will no longer work" stage. It will take longer if you're still coming to terms with everything changing. Let it. It's essential for you not to repeat this pattern of invasive co-dependence in future relationships.

What Is This Experience Teaching You?

Life-changing events happen for reasons, sometimes expected yet largely unfathomable. So, consider if this experience can provide positive learnings for you— even if in part. Maybe it is wearing you thin right now, but what if it stretches you in unexpected ways that you learn to be grateful for? What if your ex was meant to come into your life, not as a permanent fixture, but as a teacher to show you the way? I'd say these are all genuine possibilities, and you should keep your mind open.

Reflect on the lessons now open to you as you pick yourself up and dust off the trauma resulting from the separation and divorce. This education will last you a lifetime and are your saving grace from the muck of the failed marriage, except it wasn't a failure. It was a pursuit of something that would leave you with a lifetime of resilience and strength.

I know your life may feel broken right now. But even though it's not apparent at the moment, there is exquisite perfection amidst all the tiny cracks and potholes you are meandering through, powerfully and gracefully. The teachings you acquire through this experience are *necessary*. You have been saved from a life where you were a stranger to yourself. Now, you have the chance to fall in love with all that you are.

5 Tips For Rediscovering Yourself

At the onset, **revisit all the things you loved before your marriage.** Invest time in doing those things once more. If you enjoy the outdoors, go boating or golfing. Does shopping warm your soul? Visit departmental stores and experience tiny luxuries. Are you longing for creation? Take up a creative project like writing, painting, or even pottery. A time will come when it could go either way— you may love the hobby just as you did before, or even more. Or, you may find it no longer interests you. Either way, it will be time spent doing things to make *you happy*. Give life another shot as an individual, independent person.

Choose a healthy lifestyle. Exercise, eat wholesome food, spend some time outdoors, and get enough rest, and you'll be surprised at how organic healing feels. One of the primary advantages of leading a healthy lifestyle is that it might give you greater self-assurance. A good workout might help you feel more positive and euphoric by releasing hormones into your brain. Even so, regular physical activity is essential to ensure that our bodies and brains are in peak condition. We all make reasons for why we can't exercise regularly.

Yoga is a good illustration of this. It's a terrific method to get in shape without having to invest in a lot of expensive gear. The more you practice, the better you become. All the stretching helps to keep the muscles and joints supple. Moreover, you'll burn calories, which aids in weight reduction as well. To keep you looking beautiful, it's a complete exercise. I know this seems basic, but we all feel better when we are well nourished.

Try new things. This is one of my favorites. There's no better time than the lull after a divorce to take up unique activities, visit different places, experience new cuisines and meet new people. You never know when you'll chance upon something or someone you end up wanting to keep around, so try everything within the boundaries of emotional excess.

We human beings are innately curious, which is a wonderful trait we lose when responsibility weighs too heavily upon us. Trying new things is paramount to an enriched life and becoming a complete person— someone you will be proud of. It will seem challenging at the onset— no one wants to feel uncoordinated, and new events can often take time and repeatedly throw you out of your comfort zone. But the fun lies in just how messy it is. So you can scatter yourself in different directions and marvel at how completely capable you are of still retaining your inherent identity.

Every day, do something different than what you're used to, even if it's choosing a different flavor of coffee over the one you usually drink. We influence the quality of our lives and the length of our days entirely. Put another way, the more diverse and enjoyable activities you engage in, the better your life. As a result, those who seek out changing environments and actions have a better sense of well-being.

Date, but not for finding the next relationship. Your sole focus right now is on finding yourself. The more you explore different people and their varied opinions and cultural backgrounds, the deeper understanding you will form of the world and your own place in it.

Finally, **travel.** There will be occasions when you just need to get away from the routine flow of life and its humdrum beatings. It's hard to think straight following a divorce, especially if you get caught in the confines of the same place you experienced the events. So, choose an unfamiliar location within your budget, pack your bags, and let nature work her healing magic on you.

Discover how others live, and you will realize the narrow confines of your home is only an immeasurably tiny part of a far, far more extensive world. When you return, a lot will still be the same— but your perspectives will have opened, and that is just what we want.

Reconnect With Yourself

Engage in positive thoughts and always encourage healthy self-talk. If you find that you are being too harsh, stop. Replace your negative thought patterns with positive affirmations and forgive the mistakes that have occurred for all the instances that are now in the past. For example, if you find yourself thinking, "I was a fool for doing so much," change the narrative to, "I have done everything possible, and now, I choose to turn the same energy inward."

Accept every single person out there has issues of their own, and is fighting their war with nagging self-doubt and pervasive insecurities. We are no better or worse, and things will feel less dismal on realizing we're all enough just as we are. This doesn't mean you need to compare your life stage with someone else's. Let others progress as they deem fit, and reach out to help or inspire when circumstances or relationships demand it. Otherwise, be content in working on yourself and rising in your own eyes.

Cultivate positivity through your actions, and always remember to praise yourself for how far you have come. Celebrate every achievement, big and small. Even the tiniest step in the direction of self-love is a step forward, so never sell yourself short.

Be kind to your mind and body. Learn to say no to people and situations that drain you of vital joy and energy or no longer serve any wholesome purpose. You have to take ownership of your happiness. The practice of self-directed kindness and positivity will help you get to the end goal of cultivating pure and unconditional self-love. All of us can get there, and when we do, the predominant feeling will be one of profound contentment. This doesn't mean life still won't have its ups and downs. But, you will also have absolute confidence that no matter how hard the trials feel, you are stronger than them.

The connection you build with yourself will make you whole and allow others to experience you in all your glory. You will enhance each other's lives without losing yourselves, which is the point of dating after divorce. It is the only sustainable way to a fulfilling relationship where both partners are happy in themselves and willfully *choose* to keep each other joyous as well.

Get To Know The New You

Let's say you're a fascinating person you've just come across, and you'd like to know "you" better. What would you ask someone who interests you? Start with the small things, and build up from there. For instance:

- What's one redeeming quality about me?
- What's something I could work harder on?
- What makes my heart sing?
- What fuels my anger?
- Is there anyone/anything I'd go to the grave for?
- What situations undo me?
- Do I want children or step-children?
- How are my religious convictions?

- Would I like poems, chocolates, or diamonds as gifts?
- Do I work out just to be healthy, or do I enjoy it?
- Does my dream vacation look like a 5-star hotel in New York or a quaint beach hut in Bali?
- Do I enjoy cooking or prefer eating out?
- Is dancing fun or a nightmare?
- How do I feel about extreme sports like BASE jumping, parkour, or wingsuit flying)?
- Would I ever buy a $3 bottle of wine? How about a $100 bottle of wine?
- What music speaks to me— Country, Death Metal, or Pop music? None of these? Favorite musician?
- What kind of books do I enjoy? Favorite author?
- Would I rather go to a live theater or Netflix and Chill?
- Would I rather go bowling or horseback riding?
- What is an absolute dealbreaker for me in a romantic partner?
- What does my ideal Friday look like?
- What are my favorite couple things to do?
- Do I like spending weekends indoors or outdoors?

While on this adventure of self-discovery, don't make choices based on who you were during your marriage. Your past relationship is not the foundation for your present existence— so, just because your ex tried to get you to love Eminem, don't go the "I like Eminem because my ex always said he's our favorite" route. It's fine if you like him, and also okay if you don't— but the feeling should be entirely yours and not the result of old influences now gone stale.

Chapter 5
Building Trust

Trust is one of the most intricate bearings to let go of and build anew. When you trust someone, you automatically attach a bulletproof element to your relationship with them. It's another thing to know you're handling crises alone, and entirely another thing to think someone will always have your back— and then be proved wrong. You naturally don't want to make the same mistakes again, which is why one of the biggest challenges following a separation is rebuilding trust. If you've experienced trust issues before, going through a divorce can also increase your inhibitions and change how you view both other relationships and yourself.

Irrespective of why you split, divorce builds the foundation for mistrusting all existing and future relationships, even if you've never been distrusting in the past. It's easy to doubt your vulnerabilities and think, "If I made such mistakes before, I'd surely repeat them." This guilt and self-directed suspicion can manifest in how you carry yourself through subsequent relationships, especially if your marriage ends severely (with elements of infidelity attached). If you're still getting over things and you rush into new relationships, you will inevitably feel your new partner is secretive if they just keep their phone aside when you come into the room or hang up on a call too quickly.

Rushing into new relationships includes a good chance that the other person wouldn't have had the time to understand why you're seemingly paranoid about little things— such as them wanting to see a friend or coming home late from work one evening. They could begin to consider you unfit for a relationship and withdraw. Consequently, you may experience tumultuous emotions and the fear you can't hold on to love no matter how hard you try. Hence, engage in rebuilding your trust before making room for new romance in your life. Let's discuss six tips that will help.

Take It Slow

Begin by forgiving and replenishing your reservoir of faith in yourself. Trust me, after a painful divorce, the cycle of self-blame can take a while to get out of— but unless you don't, you will continue to repeat the same patterns in all future relationships. Once you have worked on yourself to the point you no longer bear the burden of self-blame, branch yourself out to healthy friendships before finally stepping into the idea of trusting someone as part of a committed relationship. When the time comes, look for eight critical components to know whether they are worthy of the faith you wish to invest in them.

Component one is **clarity**— the ability both you and your partner have to communicate with one another. You should have no qualms or questions about your expectations from the relationship. There will be certain needs, and both of you should ideally be on the same page about what and how much you can do. If you aren't ready for a particular aspect or stage, there should be absolutely clear communication. In other words, neither of you should feel "pressured" to be anything else other than your genuine selves.

The fear of losing the other shouldn't be so paramount that you once again lose your identity and become a mere follower complying to your partner's wishes. You should also be aware that we undergo significant changes following a divorce. So even if you're crystal clear about what you want today, next month, next quarter, or next year, your demands for the relationship may change, and you and your partner must be prepared to be accommodative throughout the relationship.

Then comes **compassion.** While being in love, both of you should also *care* about keeping each other's minds and souls happy. No relationship can be successful without tender-heartedness, even if different people have their own little ways of showing it. Of course, times will be there when one partner will need more understanding and kindness.

Your heart should be big enough to make space during the storms they face. I always like to think of it as this— when your partner faces a difficult situation, you don't need to save them. Rather, you need to stand by them and reinforce they have what it takes to overcome the problems at hand. And neither should they seem like a fair-weather friend— compassion is a two-way street. You cannot build trust if you're the only one showing up to anchor your partner's falls.

Our third friend is **character,** defining who we are as individual people and in relationships. Long back, I was deeply and madly in love with a boy. Everything about him spoke to something pagan in me, and I kept thinking, "for this boy, I'll change everything I have to. It doesn't matter so long as I have him by my side." And, change I did. I followed him to another city without any job. I lost my identity in the process. He wasn't one for marriage.

Minute after minute, I changed the very rubric of my nature to keep up with "having him by my side." Long story short, it was suffocating, and at one point, I had to make the difficult choice of having my heart broken till there was nothing left, or stepping away.

Fast forward to now, I know I made the right choice. If you're not behaving as you would when alone or with those who know you the best, it's not a healthy relationship. If they need you to "be a certain way" if you "want" to be with them, and this isn't who you are, girl, you need to run. It's not meant to be.

Number four in the team is **competency.** I know it sounds like an odd criteria for a relationship, but who wants to be with someone who can't even do the basics? Would you like to spend your life with a potential partner who comes in for meals, a good time, snores beside you, and then wakes up and leaves?

We expect more even from our roommates in college, and those are the times we are most likely to live like heathens. So, don't sell yourself short here, and look out for all your needs.

Your partner should be someone who knows what you like and want, and they should take pride in being able to take care of you— not because you can't do it yourself, but because all of us enjoy the feeling of security and comfort involved. Again, this is a two-way lane. You give some, you get some.

These aren't usually simple components. They need careful consideration as well as an acute awareness of how you are now feeling. However, if you are equipped with these, you will have a great starting point for determining whether or not the person or persons you are seeing (and you yourself) are appropriate for more serious relationships.

Learning To Re-Trust Someone

First things first. There should be *zero* room for misunderstandings about what you want in your post-divorce relationships. This requires absolute clear communication from your side each time— without being offbearing, of course. So, when you meet someone, it's absolutely fine to say something on the lines of, "this is what I want from life right now," not so much, "I will only go out with you if you do so and so." And it also helps you to be fair to the person you are meeting. They have a clearer understanding of whether you are looking for your next great love, or simply someone to hang out and have a good time with. Dating them should be in your best interest, and also the other way around.

How do you know if someone you're interested in is compassionate? In my experience, this takes time and careful observation. You will notice signs over time, especially by noticing how they treat others when they are stressed out. Do they take the blame for their issues out on other people? Are they always screaming and shouting profanities when they're angry? Have you noticed people being afraid to approach them? These are red flags you need to be careful of. A person who is compassionate may withdraw when they are angry or upset, but they will not make a scapegoat out of other people.

If you are in a relationship with someone, do you like who you are around them? After we take the time to honestly introspect an old marriage, we usually find that many aspects of who we were before the broken relationship has changed. The dynamics of our partnership altered us to become less than our ideal and most uplifted selves.

So, always check this bit if you see it re-emerging. I've found that even with the kindest partners, there will be those things which they intrinsically want, and we don't. Compromise will help in certain cases, but there will also be those times when you either say "no," or change your principles to agree with them. I'd always ask you to choose the first option.

If you make a decision that you yourself can't agree with, it means you're downgrading who you are. And if you can't like yourself around someone else, the relationship isn't right for you— for so many reasons, but most of all because you'll never be able to *trust them to love you for who you genuinely are.*

Masks only last for so long, and sooner or later, cracks grow and deepen till they consume you whole.

6 Tips to Build Trust Again

The first step to rebuilding trust lies in doing your homework. Choose a quiet time and place, and go into self-introspection. As yourself if the flaws in confidence are arising from your partner's or your issues, or possibly a combination of both. Before you go accusing them of something deceitful, take five deep breaths and think two important things:

- Do I choose to fight this battle?

- Is my suspicion justified?

Your gut will, in about 99% of all instances, give you a truthful answer. Learn to trust it. Turn to your intuition in times of trouble. Acknowledge your misgivings and perceptions, both of your partner as well as of potential issues in a blossoming relationship.

If there are inconsistencies between how they behave and what they say, address these problems in real-time, and maturely before you do something in haste or anger. Talk them out instead of sweeping things under the rug. Your issues aren't a shopping list to pull out once you're back home from the grocery store. You don't want them to pile up.

Accept responsibility for your part in the relationship. If you have trust-issues, you run the risk of blaming your partner for a lot of irrelevant quirks. I've been there and done it, and it's painful to go through— especially when you realize you've overreacted.

Try not to blame your partner for all issues, and consider where you can divide responsibilities. If they've done wrong and it can be redeemed, correct them. If the wrong is unforgivable, consider stepping away. And if you bear a part, no matter how big or small, acknowledge and work on navigating through it.

You may not always want to but listen to their side of the story before you project your misgivings upon them. If you've decided to talk it out, please ensure both sides of the relationship get their say in the matter without the other person headbutting in and putting words in each other mouths. When responding, try to keep your purpose in mind— are you planning to get them to feel miserable, understand where they went wrong, explain something, or simply enhance how you communicate? Fit your response to suit your purpose(s).

Don't rush into thinking whenever your partner slips up, they made an intentional mistake. All of us are human, and therefore none of us can claim flawlessness. Trust is there to help you be more open and giving towards each other, so always look for ways to forgive. If something is irritating you, look for solutions together rather than projecting it as their inadequacy, or saying things that may look like emotional blackmail, for example— "maybe it's my fault for expecting..." A more compassionate approach to this same statement would be, "do you think we could...." If they have your back, they'll help you come to a place of mutual peace.

Finally, remember practice makes perfect. You will need to take things slowly if you want to learn to trust again. Learning to trust once again is a skill that may be developed through time; thus, you should go at your own pace and concentrate on the factors that contribute to the success of your relationship. Utilize this opportunity to transform the pain of your loss into a priceless learning and development opportunity for yourself.

It makes you smarter and more aware of those who deserve you in your life and those who do not when you go through the difficulties of a failed marriage as a result of a breach of trust in the relationship. You can learn to trust your instincts and judgments, even if they have been broken in the past, if you learn how to deal with your fears head-on. If you are ready to move on to the next stage of your life, have faith in your ability to find someone who is worth the investment of your time and energy.

Chapter 6
Be Kind To your Mind

Here is the plain, unflavored truth. The person you date should be thankful to have you in their life, just as you are. At this stage, I assume you feel ready to step out and fall in love with someone else. Or, you could also be willing to test the waters. Whatever route you choose, it should add value to your life. The person or people who gain access to you from now on must be able to handle being with you.

Life is handcrafted and I wish I had recognized that in the lead-up to the divorce and during the divorce. When you handcraft a thing, there are dents and cracks, and sometimes, the thing crumbles.

In the middle of our hardship, it's hard to see that these things happen in all lives. No one escapes. Sometimes, you hammer it out or glue it in. If it doesn't work, you start all over again with acceptance and patience. And the faith that you are out of a pattern of inundated toxicity.

I used to love watching F.R.I.E.N.D.S when I was growing up. Toward the later episodes, when two of my favorite characters fall in love, one of them asks the latter (after being told off for being too prissy) if they're too high-maintenance. Their partner replies along the lines of, "yes, but I like maintaining you." That's what we're going for.

Whoever you choose to share your life with ought to align with your overall path and respect your established boundaries. There's no room for letting anyone wreck your sanity like the first time. This time, you know what you are doing.

Remember, this man will look deep within you and understand what you perceive as "imperfections." They will have their own quirks, and many of them won't make sense to you. Yet, they will destroy any lingering fears and reservations you cling to and make all of it *easy.*

You've been in a hard, complicated relationship and experienced the kind of love that takes and takes and gives you nothing in return. It has left you with years of therapy and core-shaking self-doubt. This is the love that should just fit.

There will be no pressure to be anything else other than who you are. The acceptance will shake you to your core and help you understand— *here is the man who will keep my mind and heart safe. The man who will respect my freedom and be there to share the good and the bad.* Trust me; this person is out there. But we get so swayed by our perceptions of toxic relationships. Too many of us make an ideal suit of what to expect in a man.

We forget to account for kindness, compassion, the ability to laugh, and general positivity. Instead, we choose looks, money, fame, and on another trajectory, souls impossibly different from our own with the conviction, "I'll prove how indispensable I am to them."

The truth is, in a healthy relationship, *there is nothing to prove. You're not fighting a war here.* So, the new relationships that come your way should show you love doesn't have to be dressed in the suit you made when you were twenty and impassioned by the idea of needing to kill yourself for it. It will simply knock on your door irrespective of how long it takes for you to answer. Time and again, it will reinforce how right it is, and you won't need to seek validation. *You'll just know.*

The Yin Yang Philosophy

Maybe one of the most bittersweet learnings this life will give you is that you need to truly learn what love isn't before you can make sense of what it is. And you have. You've spent your youth and years learning. But now, at this time, you have the chance to experience some of the best relationships in your life. Not only are you ready for love, but love is also ready for you.

Love should no longer feel like a ravaging storm. Instead, it should encompass the quiet peace of the morning after. It should hold you like a warm blanket and go down your throat like a soothing beverage, a reminder of all things simple and infinitely precious. Most of all, it should show you why your marriage did not work and teach you to turn your compassionate gaze inward.

So, what should you truly avoid when it comes to dating after divorce? Are there any specific pitfalls to look out for? The answers to these questions will vary depending on your core values— which is why it is important for you to choose a partner who will align with you and be the yin to your yang.

The truth is, relationships are darned tricky, no matter the ages of the parties involved. Even if you keep all your senses open, they can merge into one convoluted amoebic mass that makes you question everything.

Love has a way of contradicting everything we feel with profound intensity— and this is because we, as people, are truthfully very slippery at times. Not all of us say what we mean or mean what we say, and some of us are not good at finding words to express the language of our souls.

When developing a new alignment with someone, you have to look beyond the superficiality of words and consider the energy you feel when you are around this person.

The principle behind Yin Yang is a core component of Taoism, its inherent entity represented by "wholeness." As a philosophy, it brings peace and harmony into your life by balancing energies. Two opposites complete each other in the endeavor to form one.

When joined together, they produce something known as *chi,* which indicates being in a complete state of equilibrium. The philosophy believes everything in our world is comprised of an infinite cycle of two forces that, while opposite, complement each other. Consider the interpretation—

- Life and death,
- North and south,
- Sun and moon,
- Male and female,
- Dark and light,
- Positive and negative,
- Cold and hot.

An important thing to remember here is that all of us need yin and yang forces within us— not simply as external energies to feed into and heal our systems. Female energy (yin) is not the sole domain of a woman, and neither is male power (yang) the sole property of a man.

You have these forces at play in you— authority, femininity, decision-making, vulnerability, pragmatism, compassion, and so forth. There is a balance between these components. The more this balance, the greater you are in alignment with yourself.

So, we hold both masculine and feminine energies in our vibrational systems, and one power naturally predominates over the other. For instance, I know I am a dominant yin personality. While I reason at times, I am instinctively intuitive, contemplative, and creative. My yin: yang balance would come in at a ratio of 60:40. And that's fine. What isn't good is having a percentage that's at extreme ends— like 70:30 or 90:10.

My yang practicality helps motivate the creative aspects of yin into action and ensures I don't go emotionally overboard when times are tough. This balance influences the quality of all my intimate relationships. So, because my predominant energy is yin, *I always gravitate towards people who have more yang in them— but this doesn't mean I'll choose someone who is entirely yang and has no balance.* Let me explain.

Your energy may be mostly yang. Which isn't me saying you're a man, rather, you operate on a plane driven by rational values over people who have their heads in the clouds. Your ideal partner, in that case, should be able to balance out this predominant yang energy in you by helping you to connect with your emotional self.

On the other hand, you don't want someone who has too much yin and is constantly emotional. This will inevitably make a connection between the two of you difficult after a point, and you will be drained thinking you aren't doing enough to keep the spark alive. In other words, someone with a 60:40 yin to yang ratio should choose a 40:60 yin to yang ratio partner, not a 30:70 one. Remember, balance is key.

Finding A Balanced Relationship

How do you know a person is balanced? We tend to believe balance means two halves of one whole. On the other hand, I think it's absolutely fine for one half to be slightly dominant over the other. However, it is crucial not to overwhelm the other half completely. I may be emotional, but this aspect of my nature should not get the better of all my decision-making abilities and make me cry whenever I have to make tough choices.

When you single out a partner or even look for new friends, you need to look for key components in them. These will help you understand whether (irrespective of tiny hiccups here and there) you have the possibility of a balanced relationship to evolve.

The first key element is **trust. Trust builds a safe space where you can rely on each other.** You should be completely comfortable on the nights your partner is out, whether it's work or meeting friends. Likewise, your partner should have unshakable faith in your actions and heart. This makes your relationship strong enough to weather storms and sail through good times.

Trust will also help you solve mutual issues. If something goes wrong, you'll be safe in the knowledge they would not willingly hurt you. This will give you the leverage you need to talk things through.

The second important element is **time.** We live in a busy age, and all of us have our preoccupations. Regardless of how demanding our independent lives are, your partner and you should share the same ideals when it comes to spending time with each other.

A lot of us make the mistake of thinking we can just spend more time together when "things settle down" or "life isn't so busy." In truth, we only get more and more distant from our partners the second we begin living by this norm.

Additionally, we make the error of taking them for granted and assuming they'll stick around despite our unavailability. Both of you should set aside quality time to go on dates and share sweet moments of intimacy on a daily, weekly, and monthly basis. It doesn't have to be for hours.

Even forty minutes before bedtime, just being alone and talking about your day or appreciating their company can work wonders. I have regular spa evenings with my partner where we don't even speak, just take time to give each other massages or head rubs. The important thing is being in and enjoying each other's presence.

The third valuable component is **money.** It's a touchy subject, so much so many couples push it under the rug and think, "I don't need to talk about it so long as it's enough." Truthfully, disagreements over finance will pop up from time to time, but if you never talk about them, you run the constant risk of overspending or messing up on budgeting for essentials.

You need to coexist within the limits of what you make. Whatever your spending and saving plans are, they should work harmoniously for the both of you— and this can only happen when finance talk is approachable.

Coming in at number four is **work ethic.** If you appreciate a hard worker, you will not be comfortable in the long-run dating someone who professes to be content spending family money and just "getting by."

If you have ambition, you may think that someone who takes "life as it comes" is charming and refreshing at the onset, but you will tire out very quickly when bills pile up, and there's no respite in sight because your partner is still "discovering themselves."

All of us have different work ethics, and that is fine. But, don't build a home with someone you can't see eye-to-eye with on these things because they pile up into mountain-high frustrations. Your goals may be largely different. You may be seeking corporate success, and they may be a family man.

At the core of it, however, both of you should have a common end— be it seeking a good future for your family, or enjoying each other's successes.

The next element is **family planning.** Many of us want kids, many already have them, and many would prefer to parent pets instead. Personally, I feel all these routes are absolutely fantastic so long as your partner is on the same page with you. Don't go into a relationship with someone who says they don't want children with a latent belief that you'll be able to change their mindset.

For one, that's not the right way to think. Besides, both of you are at a mature stage in life where you have your ideals. If you can't agree on core principles, your relationship will bear the brunt of unnecessary friction.

Too many of us have children and then realize our spouse's idea of parenting is absolutely different from ours. Case in point is a friend of mine who thought her ex-husband would make a wonderful father, only to find later on that he just wanted to be around for the "cute moments," not the "yucky ones." You don't need that kind of energy in your life.

Finally, and this is something we often forget to account for— consider your attachment with people **external** to your relationship. It's fine if you're an introvert and he just needs to be around big groups of people to exist, but at no point should it feel as if you're being thrust into associations that make you uncomfortable.

So, a balance between an introvert and an extrovert should be organic. The same applies to your larger family. Both of you should be on a clear plan as to how often you meet relatives or spend time with them.

They should respect your space and need for solitude just as much as you should respect their need for an external company. If the idea of them hanging out with friends makes you icky, don't date them and make them miserable. And if they try to do the same with you, run as far as you can.

Remember you are in this together, so try to always invest in a relationship where you feel seen and heard— not just loved. Love will give your soul a home. The others— respect, value, trust, friendship, compromise— will ensure this home is *permanent.*

Now that you know the elements to balance a relationship, you may be wondering how you can spot red flags when you just begin dating. This is what we will explore in detail in the next chapter.

Chapter 7
Recognizing The Red Flags

Red flags are scary. You're out there, enjoying the company of someone wonderful when they suddenly do or say something that completely goes against your core philosophy. We crave connection with others; indeed, it is one of the most integral parts of our lives. We love feeling loved, but problems start appearing when this feeling encompasses our ability to understand when specific behavior patterns are becoming harmful to us and those around us— like our children.

Not all relationships improve our lives. Some relationships damage our well-being, and we recognize the harm they have caused far too late. Red flags in relationships are warning signs indicating unhealthy and manipulative behavior. They may not be recognizable all the time, especially if you are wearing those sepia-tinted love goggles which makes you blind to any wrongs your partner may commit. But, be mindful that manipulative behavior patterns tend to magnify and become more and more problematic over time.

I'd say the best you can do to steer clear of red flags is to be aware of what you are getting into before committing to a person. Subtle red flags, which can be measured through tricky phrases like, "you're too good for me," or being extra-possessive about how you dress and who you meet (which many of us make the mistake of considering adorable at the onset), can be signs of victimization, narcissism, and toxic dependency.

When warning signs arise in a relationship, it's a good opportunity to take stock of the dynamics between you and the other person. Malignant conduct is often imperceptible and gradual. It sneaks up on us when we're at our weakest, and if we're not careful, it may take over our life. A chain reaction of injuries to ourselves and the people around us is possible. The best way to protect ourselves from potentially harmful situations is to increase our knowledge of warning signs and poisonous conduct.

Red flags may appear at any time in a relationship, but they are most prevalent in the beginning. If you work on honing your intuition, you'll be able to pick up on things faster. Without even knowing it, your date is probably waving the red flag. Next time you're out on a date or talking on the phone in preparation for one, listen carefully to what is said and what isn't. If something isn't sitting quite right with you, that's valuable information.

What Is A Dating Red Flag?

Does everything seem fine during a conversation with a potential date, and then they say something that degrades you, ever so subtly? Many years back, I went out on a date with a man who seemed perfect. He was well-dressed and behaved like a gentleman. He reached my house on time, held all doors open without jabbering about "independent women can open their own doors," and talked with courtesy.

Over our dinner, everything he said sat well with me. As things were winding down, he finally leaned back in his chair and cast an admiring look before claiming, "*I'd really like to take you out and make you mine. You look like a girl who needs protecting, and I'd hate for you to keep putting yourself out there and getting hurt.*" His statement was in earnest, and it made me think.

I was too stumped to respond immediately, but I'd learned my lessons about reacting too quickly. I went home and mulled over his words, and decided they posed a red flag for me. So, here's the thing. Whatever a potential partner says may not turn out to be a red flag for someone who desires just what they are offering.

However, if you are someone independent and on a journey of reclaiming yourself, it is highly toxic for someone to come along and tell you they want to date you so you don't have to bother with "putting yourself out there." In other words, there will be occasions where red flags are subjective.

Overall, though, any particular word, gesture or action that makes you question the other person's motives as well as communicates a lack of respect and integrity for who you are and where you come from is a potential red flag. Some of these toxic traits include:

- A date who can do nothing except talk about themselves.

- Being overly occupied with avoiding any serious conversation.

- Sharing too much about the ex and their dynamic with them.

- Displaying an overall coldness and withholding affection because "they've been hurt in the past."

Red flags in romantic relationships become dangerous because the longer you ignore them and sweep them under the rug, the more you view them as "part of the package." You think the good comes with the bad— so what if your partner is a compulsive liar? They love you and they'll change if you show them you're going to stick around— right? Unfortunately, that isn't how it works. The more you show a liar you'll put up with his ways no matter how worse the lies get, the more adept they'll become at lying. The only people who end up suffering are you, and in most cases, also your children.

With this being said, red flags can pop up in a number of circumstances. It would be useful to break them down and look at them one by one.

General Dating Red Flags

In the world of dating, red flags can cruise right up the line of "abusive behavior" and sometimes even waltz all over it. Before you're certain of what's going on, you're being led into a dangerous tango, so it's pretty essential for you to know what you're getting yourself into. When you start dating, always keep an eye out for these potential pitfalls that could spell trouble later on.

Love Bombing

Ever been on a date where you're showered with over-the-top displays of affection and attention? Did it seem slightly unreal? This is love bombing, or in other words, your potential love interest's sneaky attempt to influence you to get with them by showing you how much they have to offer. Examples of love bombing include:

- Exorbitant gifts too often and too soon,

- Excessive (often unreal) compliments,

- Wanting to be near you all the time,

- Texting, calling or emailing you multiple times in a day—often when you're busy with work and other important things,

- Mirroring and copying all your interests,

- Demanding you spend more time with them rather than family or friends,

- Constantly pining for taking things to the next level—such as asking you to move in with them a month into the relationship, and

- Oddly excessive interest in your life, background and interests.

The purpose of love bombing is to make you feel as if there is no one else in the world who knows and loves you as much as they do. You become far more receptive to doing whatever they ask you, which is just where they need you to be. So, you end up sharing intimate details of your past and all your struggles. They keep notes of everything to use against you later.

You're telling them of all the abuse and neglect you endured in your last relationship. On the surface, They seem to be offering their full empathy to ensure emotional and physical intimacy. Unbeknownst to you, it's going to come back in arguments via dialogues like, *"You remember this went wrong in your last relationship, right? I don't want the same thing to happen,"* or *"you've been too damaged to think clearly,"* or *"haven't you learned anything from the mistakes you made before,"* and so it goes on.

Remember a general rule of thumb— if it seems too good to be real, it most often is. All the attention and over-the-top praise may seem wonderful at the onset, but trust your gut if you feel it's illusory.

Disrespect For Your Boundaries

All of us have distinct sexual, mental and physical boundaries. The beginning parts of a relationship should devote enough time to exploring these as a couple. When you start dating someone new, you take time to understand what constitutes their ethics, principles, and limitations in a healthy way so that each of you feels safe, respected, and committed to progressing further. If the person you date is coercing or pressuring you into bending your boundaries, it can be a major early red flag in the relationship.

So, if they make requests like asking for an extra hour when you've told them you have kids waiting for you to come home, understand it isn't right, no matter how giddy they make you feel. Likewise, if that kiss or touch feels too invasive, or if they constantly ask intimate questions and encroach your personal space, they're messing with what makes you *you*. These are early signs of disrespect and disregard for your feelings, and it's not something you want to put up with in the long or even short run.

Obsessive Check-Ins

All of us enjoy the feeling of having people watch over us. The occasional, "just checking in to make sure you're doing good" message can warm up an otherwise rainy day. But, if these messages start pouring in, and from the same person, every hour— you can bet you've got yourself a red flag. It's such a fine line here, which is why it's doubly important for you to understand when their messages feel like overstepping boundaries.

Do they keep texting when you're out with friends or busy with work? Do they get excessively upset if you're out later than you reckoned if you've already established you are not in a committed, exclusive relationship? Do they shout and cause scenes when you come back a little late from a family gathering?

If the checking in reaches a stage where it feels like they're trying to act like a living, breathing GPS tracker, know you deserve better than this relationship. A time will come when they won't even trust you when you're at home or in the bathroom for too long. It's getting suffocated in real time, one day after the next.

They Crave Prioritization

At the very onset of a relationship, when things are light and fun, meeting up shouldn't feel like a burden. Each of you should know that you're spending time by way of getting to know the other, and not as a priority. As a matter of fact, you don't want to overspend time or overshare information from the get-go. It should be a gradual unfolding, where prioritizing their place in your life happens eventually and because of the connection you develop.

If someone is always pushing for you to place them first, they are either desperate for your attention and desire that you sacrifice your own happiness for their own, or they are trying to take up as much of your time and mental space as possible at the price of your own well-being.

A week or even a month into a new relationship, if your partner is constantly asking you to ditch plans with friends and family and share that time with them instead, it's a definite red flag. Plus, if they keep butting into other things you enjoy doing with friends or your relatives— like going out shopping or having a movie night with the kids, they are definitely wading too thin. Suppose you invite them on your own accord, it's different. However, if they force you into a situation where you can't do anything except ask them to tag along, it's an early sign of trouble in paradise.

They're Excessively Jealous

Partners who are distrustful of all your friends and relatives generally suffer from a combination of anger, anxiety, deep-seated insecurity issues, and fear. This toxic cocktail of emotions comes through in a relationship that can seem very passionate at first, but quickly grows into a suffocating nightmare.

It's fine to be envious at times— we all have days when we think, "wow, my partner looks so good, I'll bet all the women are going to have eyes for him tonight," but there's a vast difference between that and yelling the house down at your partner because he looks good. In other words, there's a clear boundary separating healthy envy from absolute jealousy.

If your potential romantic interest s doing any of these things, you need to watch out:

- Gets angry whenever you share memories of happy incidents that happened before or don't involve them,

- Bring up arguments whenever you hang out with friends,

- Get very defensive when you discuss healthy boundaries or your past relationships,

- Badmouth your family and friends,

- Constantly berate you and make you feel diminished, and

- Display toxic anger whenever someone approaches you in a public setting.

They Make Fun Of You

If a potential romantic interest is making offhand comments about you (even in jest) at the onset, it could be a telling red flag. These comments could be about how you dress, the music you like, the food you enjoy, your talking habits, and your career choices.

When anything they say, whether or not it is a trifle to them, hurts you, you reserve the right to get up and walk out before the relationship doubles in toxicity. Consequentially, if they understand and try to make amends, the relationship has hope. If, however, they say things like, "why can't you take a joke?" or "you're being too serious," get out of there because you deserve better.

They Like To Keep Their Exes Close

Dear God. I once met a man who was seemingly perfect. But, he had a girlfriend who kept demanding that he return to her. And I thought it would fizzle out, but a time came when I saw he kept adding fuel to the fodder. He'd say "I love you" to her and tell me he meant it as a friend. He'd go over to her place with the argument "he wanted to give her closure." And she kept blaming me for the pitfalls in their relationship— although I met him long after they had ceased to be a couple. Whatever you do, DO NOT get into a relationship with a man like this.

On the other hand, many people may maintain healthy relationships with their exes, especially if they are coparenting children together. You'll know at the early phase if something seems off about how they treat you when their ex is around, or how they speak about their ex. Their respecting and caring for their ex should never come at the cost of compromising your relationship with them, so if that feels like the case, don't indulge them.

Displaying Inconsistencies

If both of you are fine with taking things slow and not being exclusive, it's fine. But, if you clearly expect a monogamous relationship, and they keep treating you as one option among many, it's not great news. You're not participating in a competition here. Are they always falling short on their promises? Inconsistent conduct is an indication of immaturity as well as a lack of trustworthiness; it may also suggest that they do not value you for what you are capable of offering. It's possible that they are still unclear about whether or not this is the right romantic partnership for them, and that they are also considering other options.

The fact that they alter their conduct depending on who they are speaking with is another evidence that they cannot be trusted. Pay attention to how they behave with other people, especially if they approach one person in a specific manner but act quite differently around others.

Your Friends Are Iffy About Them

There's a good reason why you keep in touch with the people you do. One common reason is that you have a lot in common philosophically and personally. Therefore, it might be a significant red signal if your friends don't approve of your new love interest.

When you're too near to a person, you may not be able to pick up on the vibrations they're giving out.

When it comes to a good friend, you can always expect them to give you the truth, even if it hurts. In the event that your new partner is downright cruel, harsh, or inconsiderate to your friends, you should most definitely part ways with them.

You Dislike Their Company When They're Sober

Some people can be the life of the party. They make you feel warm, loved, and oh-so-giddy. The only thorn in their perfect get-up is they need a few drinks in them before they can impress you. I'd say, always go on a few no alcohol dates to understand if you vibe with who the person is outside of the booze buzz. Plus, if they like the drinks a little too much, you need to be careful.

Alcohol abuse can ruin any relationship— even ones that are otherwise very strong. The same applies to any form of abuse involving unmentionables. Be careful what you get yourself into, because this is you taking another chance on love and romance. You deserve peace, not the added trauma of managing an addict.

Your Gut Feeling Tells You To Run

Girl, if the stomach says "no," you scatter as fast as you can go. I apologize for the awful poem, but I mean it. Most of the time, your intuition will sense things your eyes cannot. So, if there's anything that makes you feel there's a slight issue with the person you're seeing, reconsider hanging out with them.

Even if your gut instinct is wrong, you may carry it indefinitely, which adds up to your own insecurities and feeds into the relationship you build. It could also be a sign you aren't ready to begin dating yet. Whatever it is, respect where you are at in this stage of life, and if it feels like you're not in the presence of the right person for you, don't compromise.

Online Dating Red Flags

Laggy video calls, lack of physical touch, and the awkward random internet outages may all make dating problematic. Online dating can be challenging. On the other hand, it may become much more complicated than that. Is it possible for you to have faith in the other person on the other end of the line? Look out for these warning signs while using online dating services to help keep you safe.

They're Constantly Asking For Money

Are you fond of Netflix documentaries? I swear, I don't watch them all the time, but there are days when I like nothing better than kicking back with a tub of popcorn and a comfy blanket covering me as I watch other people coming to terms with horrifying things happening to them— all because they trusted the wrong people.

Time and again, a theme of these documentaries (case in point being *The Tinder Swindler*) lies in beautiful, capable, yet insecure women giving their all-in to a stranger online. They spend exorbitant amounts of money on this stranger, absolutely believing it when they say, "I have the money, I just can't access it right now. I'll pay you back soon." And this goes on and on till the debt collection calls come pouring in.

So, no matter how sincere an online date may seem, *never* give money to someone you've met on a dating app. It doesn't matter if they appeal to your vulnerabilities or it seems as if they genuinely need help. If the sum is exorbitant and seems unusual, *don't fall for it.* You don't want to be looking at the end of a long scam where you find that you've borrowed immense amounts from your bank to help out a con artist, to the point you have absolutely nothing left to rebuild your life.

It's true that all of us may run into financial issues from time-to-time but think. Would you be comfortable borrowing money from a man you've just met? No! This is why boundaries are so important. You need to understand that early on in a relationship, apart from sharing bills or paying for dinners (depending on your comfort about this), you do not need to loan your date money! As a matter of fact, it's a very slippery slope that you should avoid getting on at all costs, because the risks involved are usually too dangerous.

They Constantly Deprecate Themselves

If you find yourself in the middle of a relationship where the man is constantly apologizing and making self-derogatory jokes about their "bad drinking habits" or "rude behavior" but doing nothing to fix it, then get out of this online chat nightmare as soon as you can. Chances are they're not interested in fixing what's negative about them at all, and they also want you to understand they'll be this way for an indefinite period— possibly forever.

Whenever you do try to point it out, they'll likely sway you to their side with the, "I'm going to try harder/ why can't you understand how difficult it is for me/ you deserve better" excuses, with their sole intent being manipulating you into remaining in a perpetual status quo.

They're Too Quick With The "I Love You"

Let's face it. One of the biggest plus and minus points of online dating is how quickly it allows you to develop intimacy. The feeling of light-headedness stems from the ease with which you can mold your personality online to show and reveal only those aspects of yourself that will make you the most appealing to the people you target. And this can be quite risky, especially since we make the mistake of taking these aspects for real. It also brings forward the very real danger of inauthenticity, because love lies in knowing all the little quirks of a human being, and knowing you don't want to live without them nonetheless.

When you're dating someone online, the sensible thing is to wait until you have a proper chance at a face-to-face meeting, or, the way I see it, at least a few of them. You should get to experience the person in their living, breathing reality— and not the mere parts they display for your benefit online. If you find someone telling you they love you when you're just getting to know them— and if it all feels too perfect, *it probably is.*

Their Profile Is Lacking Or Suspicious

Does it look like they have a celebrity's profile picture as their display? I'll admit, I do like the ones with anime displays because they help me understand whether the people I'm talking to grew up on Studio Ghibli films like I did. But, as you talk with them, they should be absolutely open to sharing their pictures with you. Their profile shouldn't look like a desert— in that, there should be people interacting with their posts, updates, and pictures, even if these are sparse or scattered.

If you open a picture and find a number of random comments on it that make no sense and look like they've been generated by one of those "fake follower/ fake comments and likes" applications, know that you've encountered someone who is shady. And if you didn't find them on social media sites like Instagram or Facebook and instead met them on a whole dating site, pictures are a must. That's the whole point behind a dating site.

If they're catfishing you, you'll know sooner or later. But you should never indulge a dating profile that looks as bare as the Sahara. Whenever possible, converse via video calls to get an understanding of the men behind the pictures.

Red Flags When Dating in Your 50s (60s and 70s)

Contrary to what many people think, you can have the most beautiful relationship of your entire life at this age. You know yourself, and the connection you've built is likely stronger than it has ever been. You also understand what to expect from others. With this being said, there are some red flags you need to be mindful of so that your new journey is as painless and sunny as it can be.

They're Apprentice Houdinis

For the love of God, do not waste this beautiful life on a flaky person. Even if you really like them, and the few dates you go on seem too good to be true, if they disappear randomly for weeks or months after that, shun them. They may come back after a period and make excuses about how busy they were, and they're at an age where they have other priorities, but no. There is a line of difference between priority and decency. Remember, you're not asking them to meet you every day. However, you have the complete right to be in the loop. If they're not talking to you for weeks after a date, find someone better to move on to.

They Live On Their Keypads

For the introverts among us, texting is like a boon to our existence. However, when you are dating someone, even if they abhor calls or meet in person, they must take out some time— at least every few days, to call or meet up with you. Texting can be very impersonal, and I've found that it's also very difficult to convey certain messages without coming across as offensive or rude because of, well, *tone*.

You need to be able to meet up for important conversations and even the tiny, silly things like experiencing movie nights and sunsets together. The whole point of falling in love is to wade through life's little glories and dips with each other, and trust me when I say you can't experience this via text messages.

They're Constantly See-Sawing Between Their Priorities

In our midlife periods, we are extremely busy at times. Work commitments come in the way, along with children, grandchildren, and other family needs. So, it makes sense that we may not have as much time to lavish on our significant other as we'd like. But, this is not an excuse for someone to treat you like seconds at a meal when they're not full enough.

You deserve respect and their time, and I always believe that five minutes to call someone at the end of the day to talk about how life has gone is not that hard— especially if you are in love with them. If they profess to be in love with you and yet cannot be bothered to keep in touch, you should aim for far better.

They're Stuck In NeverLand

We've all met men who expect us to mother them from time-to-time. Who can never seem to find their socks or burn their hands when trying to heat a meal in the microwave. To an extent, it's understandable because men do tend to have their minds scattered on a number of things. What isn't okay is for them to rely on you for every tiny thing— from folding and washing their clothes, to cooking their meals, and also waking them up and getting them ready for the office.

I've noticed emotional maturity has no direct correlation with physical age. Many people remain stuck in the whirlpool of emotionally toxic codependent habits from their youth. They may try to put a dazzling "I need you and love you, so I depend on you" suit upon their neediness, but you are not their housekeeper, nurse, or mother. You are their partner. If they cannot live up to basic expectations, you know you have yourself a red flag.

Red Flags In Dating A Divorced Man

Chances are, once you have waded the waters of marriage, love and dating for a while, you will encounter a divorced man. And they can be just who you need. Men who have gone through pain and struggle that parallels your own will understand what you are looking for, and what you expect from life in general. However, you must also understand that we deal with a lot of emotional baggage with the demise of a marriage. So, if you are dating a divorced man and these red flags show up, think twice before going too hard too soon.

The Trash Talker

Unresolved hurt and anger can be serious detriments to building a fruitful, beautiful new relationship. If the man you are going out with someone who is constantly badmouthing their ex, there's a good chance they are not emotionally prepared for a new relationship. It will be very hard for you to navigate a relationship where the other person still has so many unresolved feelings about their ex.

If they speak with impassioned hate, it's likely they're still deeply invested in them, and cannot get over how they were hurt. This means latent love for the ex, major trust issues, and a world of pent-up anger. You've gone through your own struggle to come to this stage. I'd advise you to think twice before committing to someone who makes you go through the entire battlefield all over again.

The "It's Not Me, It's Them!"

All of us would like to believe our own parts in the divorce are not as weighty as the mistakes made by our partners. But, maturity lies in realizing that we all contribute in some way or the other to what crumbles. Of course, the distribution of things that didn't work doesn't have to be an even fifty-fifty. But a very important aspect in getting out (and I mean truly out) of the baggage surrounding a divorce is knowing where you went wrong, and taking the onus of it.

I'll share an example. One of my dear friends was subjected to constant mental abuse by her husband. He never lifted a hand on her, but the verbal onslaught he subjected her to was debilitating. He didn't leave anyone– her friends, family, children –all of them were subjected to his cussing and rudeness. For years, I watched her make excuses for him. And this was not good. It meant she stuck up for his faults and to an extent, also gave him the room and space to misbehave even more.

We told her time and again to stop before things got worse, but again, you cannot reason with someone who will not hear you. Ultimately, things came to a standstill when he took his rage out on their daughter. So, his fault was infinitely larger, but she wasn't blameless.

In the same way, I've had my own issues with my marriage. We all do things that we'd be wise not to repeat in future associations, so if you go out with someone who unequivocally says they had no fault in things going wrong, and everything crumbled because of their ex-partner, you'd be wise to be wary. Taking responsibility is one of the toughest jobs you'll do in this life, but you cannot navigate through everything by simply putting responsibilities on everyone else's shoulders. Just as they blame their ex now, they will look for and find multiple reasons to blame you for trivialities.

Their Sarcasm Is Hurtful

Whenever I seek new company, I pay attention to their ability to not take life too seriously. They should be able to laugh at themselves and understand that embarrassing situations happen to all of us. But, if the sarcasm is growing, and in unwarranted ways, you should be careful.

If you become the brunt of their jokes, and they pass crude and mean comments about your weight, how you dress, or how you carry yourself and even the more general things like your friends and family, do not indulge them. The negativity you become privy to can paralyze the relationship and take a toll on your mental health. Plus, they have absolutely zero right to get in laughs at the expense of derogating you. You're worth much more and far better than that.

They're Always Distrustful

Finally, if the divorcee constantly doubts your actions, raising questions about where you are and what you are doing, or bothering you multiple times in a day because they don't believe you when you tell them you're busy, the relationship isn't good for you.

I once went out with a man who was as sweet as anything. Everything felt right, until he began demanding pictures whenever I would go out. His logic was this was a way of keeping track of me, so I'd be safe, but we both knew what his intentions were. Things reached a standstill when he put a tracking application on my mobile without my consent. You don't want it to go as far as that.

Men, and to be honest, any human being like this, will constantly try to bring you down and blame you for everything you try to do as an independent individual. You don't want that burden in your life – not after what you have already endured.

Dating A Widower Red Flags

Falling in love with a person who has experienced profound loss is a different experience. They have experienced different stages of grief, mourning and letting go. In marriages where the only point of separation lies in the physicality of death, you are meeting someone who has experienced deep love, and had to let go of it because there was no other option. It can enrich you, but if you aren't ready, you may find yourself becoming overwhelmed. For your own preparedness, keep these red flags in mind so that you don't end up shouldering something you're not ready for.

They're Reluctant To Heal

It may seem as if they have no time for you except when physical need or the desire to have someone to vent to becomes too much. This could be a sign that they've martyred themselves for the sake of the person they loved, and being stuck as they are, they're not interested in moving on. If this is their path, and you force yourself to walk on it, you'd be giving up on everything you have hoped for at this second shot in love. Ask yourself whether you're okay with just being a tissue to wipe tears, or a friend for troubled times. If you're looking for more, know this isn't the right relationship for you.

They're Living In Their Memories

You may find odd differences in how they treat you. There are days when it feels as if they're completely in love, and then there are others where it's as if you are competing with a ghost. And you can't do that. If their minds are stuck in the land of memories, and they aren't willing to make room for you, the relationship will eventually fizzle out. There's only so much of a hurricane that you can bear, especially after your own journey of loss and healing.

Consider this point carefully. Yes, the lovey-dovey days may seem sweet and healing, but does it make up for the ones where you feel as if you're talking to a broken recorder that can't hear, see, or feel you? And if yes, are you willing to endure this dichotomy for the rest of your life?

They're Too Reclusive, And Not In The Good Way

Hey, if both of you are introverts and you like nothing better than snuggling up in your home with drinks and good books, there's nothing like it. But if your man is otherwise social but refuses to be seen with you for various odd reasons, you need to be careful. It could be that he's afraid of what others are expecting and wants to protect you from how judgemental people can be— but that choice lies upon both of you.

Sooner or later, you have to meet his friends and family, and if he keeps making excuses to avoid introducing you to them, it's a definite red flag. When a significant other fails to connect you to their friends, family, or other people they know, either in person or on social media, this is known as pocketing.

From the outside looking in, your connection doesn't seem to exist. If he flat-out says no, there's no use in pleading; he just doesn't want to meet you. He'll simply dislike you for pushing him too soon, and you'll be irritated that he doesn't want to share his people or life with you. In the end, you shouldn't have to badger him into including you.

Someone who is ready to fall in love and is sincere will be eager to include you in his inner circle. As soon as word of you spreads, everyone he knows will be smitten, and his love for you will only grow. You shouldn't settle for a person who is indifferent to your natural need to be familiar with people he is close to. For this reason, it's important to ensure that he feels the same way about you before deciding whether or not to let him into your life.

Dating A Narcissist Red Flags

Narcissists typically seem to have it all on paper: a successful profession, plenty of money, a dazzling personal life, and a slew of admirers. You may even wonder how you got so lucky to end up with someone who's just so perfect and has every quality you've ever dreamed of in a partner.

Discard this notion, though, since daydreaming about such a partner might put you in an unfavorable position. The dynamics of a partnership with a narcissist are more nuanced. Narcissists believe that the only people who can really appreciate them are themselves and that they, in turn, deserve to be surrounded by other individuals who are also exceptional. If the following warning signs seem too vivid, even if you're off to what seems like a terrific start, be cautious.

They Love Bomb You

Love bombing is a tactic of manipulation that's textbook to narcissists. They issue an avalanche of affection within a few days of meeting you. The flow of such good emotions makes you feel overwhelmed, and you make the mistake of thinking you are finally getting the love and acceptance you deserve. You believe you've met someone truly invested in you.

Then, slowly, they begin withdrawing this affection bit by bit until one day, they seem cold and harsh. You remain stuck in the memories of how good it used to be, and end up thinking you're making mistakes which leads to the downfall of the relationship. This makes you scramble to save it, and you give them whatever they desire— sex, money, or validation.

Unfortunately, the problem with love bombing is you may not find out it's happened until you're deep into the relationship. A way to know is if it feels like he's doing too much for you right off the bat. Always remember, when you're getting to know someone, it shouldn't feel as if they're a hurricane of love, passion, and gifts. Not at this age, and definitely not when you're looking for a mature relationship. Let this be the sign that you should be wary of.

They Have An Undeniable Need For Validation

They're happy with you, but only in so far as things are going just the way they want. They'll constantly need you to remind them why you're in love with them and what makes them so perfect. A time will come when they won't be interested in anything else you have to say, unless it's something good about them.

Perchance you highlight some fault in their nature, it's hell unleashed on you. But the moment you give them what they want, they'll show you the moon and stars and make you feel like you are the most indispensable person to have graced their world— even if you have known them just for a week.

They Exhibit Zero Empathy

Look for subtle signs in your relationship. Does your partner care about you having experienced a tough day at work or a low tide in life in general? Are they giving you time and space to speak and share what you've done throughout the day? Do they want to be there for you when recovering from something intense? Or are they always bored when you express things that make you feel sad?

Narcissists typically cannot experience other people's feelings or the tide of emotions that can pass through them. So, they are never able to understand the nuances of the world lying beyond their own narrow perspectives. The grandiose displays of affection water down after a point, and you feel you are no longer seen, understood, or accepted. This is a major red flag and one that you do not want in your life.

They Gaslight You

Finally, if it feels like the onus of every tiny mistake happening in a relationship is all your fault, run as fast as you can. You're being gaslit into staying; the longer you commit, the worse it will become.

Gaslighting is a practice where your perception of reality is subjected to questions. It's very toxic because whenever you find something your partner is doing is wrong, they turn the tables on you and make you feel like it's you who is at fault instead. Over time, it makes you lose your self-confidence, and you forgo the ability to evaluate your decisions. Your gut instinct wears down to the point where you cannot do anything without checking back with your manipulative partner.

I'd say that you should always understand this new journey is supposed to be a revelation. It's foolish to expect everything will go exactly how you want it to, but our goal is to prevent anything terrible or hurtful from happening— to the extent that it takes you four steps back when you've just begun moving forward. Much of this also involves understanding intimacy, so we'll get into that in the next chapter.

Chapter 8

Recognizing Dangerous Intimacy

Getting into a new relationship, especially one which begins to feel serious, can be equal parts exhilarating and scary. There's a different kind of passion, a slower burn, and a sweet release. Along with all the emotions you are experiencing, intimacy can become a tricky terrain, given that you've shared so much of yourself with only one other person over so many years. Allowing that space and access to your body to an entirely different being may take time, and it is important that you don't rush the process.

What Is Intimacy?

I look at intimacy as I'd look at how nature opens herself up to us. Have you observed the pattern in which seasons change? There is something oddly familiar about them. Spring gives way to summer, Autumn, until one day, frost seeps in. This doesn't mean we don't experience the occasional out-of-season weather characterized by rain storms in January or an unusually chilly day in June. But, we automatically understand this is an anomaly, and that things will go back to what they were once this unexpected event passes. So also in all intimate relationships, we intrinsically understand and trust the people involved, so much so that tiny trifles in their behaviors are not enough to change our perceptions or shake our faith in them.

An intimacy of this sort, particularly in relationships where we choose people (as opposed to being born to, with, or giving birth to them) builds over time as you connect at deeper levels, grow to care about one another, and experience richer comfort in the time you spend together. It may not always involve a sexual equation— indeed, many beautifully intimate relationships are also platonic. But it always has a profound emotional depth. In romantic partnerships, it marries the two into one composite whole.

Dating someone new and falling for them can be an entirely giddy experience of intimate moments. For a few of us, it resembles a whole new kind of falling in love for the first time. It's easy to see why you may get swept away by the torrential downpour of the emotions you experience. While this happens, however, your feet need to be as close to stable ground as possible.

A very palpable danger surrounding the fear we have of intimacy has more to do with complacency. Since we've experienced an old relationship falter, we already know what it feels like to be taken for granted. Naturally, when we are intimate with a partner, we display all our vulnerabilities to them.

Once they realize they have regular access to our inherent emotional vulnerabilities, they can maneuver these as they like. The danger arises when someone who has full access ends up betraying us. If it happens in relationships following a divorce, it's like being stabbed in the heart all over again.

The other issue surrounding intimacy surrounds the topic of introducing your children to someone new. Additionally, how do you ensure safe sex following the demise of a marriage, where the whole concept of sex may have been relegated to the domain of something entirely vanilla (or unsafe)?

Therein lies the poignant irony of it all. We do strive for intimacy, but once we have it, we become afraid of it. We fall into an eternal conundrum of *"women only talk about their issues, and men don't enjoy the truth talk."* This encourages a chasm to open up wide, which in turn leads to the slow decay of the relationship.

I'd say it is important to go old-fashioned when you feel distance is taking too much space between you and someone you love. Indulge in a good old cocktail hour at the end of the day, a time where you can just unwind and discuss your thoughts without necessarily being confrontational.

Intimacy Exists Outside Of Just Sex

Here's a Venn diagram for you. Sexual intercourse includes intimacy. Intimacy, however, need not always involve sexual intercourse. I need to clarify this a little. There are sexual adventures that go beyond the realm of intimacy as well—

especially in case someone is just interested in a casual hookup. But in being with someone else, acts such as kissing the forehead or looking lovingly at each other, brushing each other's arms— and other faint indicators do point to a kind of intimacy, even if it is only fleeting.

When we think of intimacy, we often mistakenly think of sex. The two are widely considered synonymous, but they aren't one and the same. Intercourse is about as close to another human as we can physically get— or so you'd think. Intimacy goes a step further and links your mind and soul to that of another. At least four types of intimacy don't involve sex or touch but are just as impactful in a romantic partnership.

Long-term commitments usually require sustainable rapport beyond just chemistry in the bedroom. Without types of intimacy besides physical, the relationship can start to drift apart or remain at a very superficial level. As you spend more and more time with each other, you will share joys, frustrations, fears, sorrows, and long-term goals. This also means you share difficult emotions.

The key here is to find a way to do all the sharing respectfully. Of course, letting down your emotional guard can be scary at the onset, but this is more than sex. *The entire act of long-term love lies in building trust.* That is at the core of intimacy. You'll find that even silly conversations about nothing at all will bring you closer to your significant other.

Perhaps sharing the stuff of everyday life will become something you enjoy because you have someone looking forward to having you back home. On other occasions, you'll find you don't even need words to explain how you feel. There is no sex involved here— it is pure, raw emotion. And sex will never sustain a long-term relationship. Sharing yourself, your ideals, goals, dreams and tiny quirks— in other words, building intimacy, *will*.

Let's now take a look at the four kinds of intimacy that don't necessarily involve any physical closeness.

Emotional Intimacy

Emotional intimacy exists when you feel safe in the shared space between you and your partner.

It involves candid, authentic discussions surrounding your mutual thoughts and feelings. You are emotionally intimate when you can to tell each other your deepest fears, dreams, disappointments, and most complicated emotions, as well as feel seen and understood when you do.

We confide in people whom we trust— and this is the hallmark of cherishing an emotionally intimate relationship. We understand they won't always tell us what we want to hear, but we trust they won't repeat anything we share in confidence. We also don't expect them to embarrass or belittle us. Uninhibited expression defines what you two share, and in the space between you, you know that this is a man who will never give you any judgment, only guide you towards the light. What does this beautiful form of closeness look like? Let's consider a few examples:

- A couple has a lengthy and heartfelt conversation about what they want their relationship to be like in the future and what is still important to them in the present. Following the conclusion of the discussion, both feel more connected to and understand each other better.

- A man expresses that his partner maintaining relationships with exes makes him uncomfortable. His partner works to empathize with his concerns instead of making the case that he's immature or jealous.

- Following a stressful day at work, a woman returns home and opens up to her partner about everything that happened, including the emotions she didn't feel comfortable sharing with her coworkers. Her companion asks gentle, empathetic questions that affirm her feelings and aid in her processing of the experience.

- A woman confides in her spouse that she's unhappy with her body after having a baby. She trusts her partner to offer comfort and help her develop solutions if desired rather than dismiss her feelings.

- After a few months into their relationship, a woman tells her partner she was abused as a child. Their partner is attentive, takes the situation seriously, and offers emotional support as well as the conviction that they will navigate through this together, as a team.

How To Increase Emotional Intimacy

One of the most pertinent, and common lines I've heard from friends and my larger circle when it comes to maintaining long-term relationships is this: *"I love my partner, and I believe he loves me too. But he doesn't show it as much and there are days I feel like I'm not valid."* One of the fundamental (and perhaps the sweetest) parts of any romantic relationship lies in being able to share your secrets, talk openly about your relationship, and disclose news that is important to you without being afraid your partner will judge you for how you acted or what you feel. A couple is always happier when both of you can share and respect each other's feelings.

Emotional intimacy builds a profound sense of security within your relationship and empowers you to be your true, vulnerable self without feeling afraid your partner will tear you apart. It gives you the ability to be entirely yourself— pimples and cellulite and all— without constantly worrying that your tiny imperfections (which make you perfectly beautiful) will sabotage the relationship. In the absence of this intimacy, any relationship will struggle. For instance, you may find you are angry or stressed, experiencing hypersensitivity, being afraid if your partner is loyal, or feeling lonely and isolated.

You can foster emotional closeness in your relationships by engaging in deeper, more introspective conversation, talking about emotions and experiences that you don't typically share with others, and doing so on a regular basis. In a similar vein, make sure to ask your spouse some thoughtful questions and show an interest in what they think and how they feel. Listen to understand rather than being quick and judgmental in your responses. Always take care not to invalidate the other person's feelings so that you can create an atmosphere that is conducive to honest communication and open dialogue.

Intellectual Intimacy

A good partner cares for you and respects what you bring to the relationship, irrespective of any differences in how you think, express, or act. Comfort with communicating beliefs and viewpoints without worrying about potential conflicts creates intellectual intimacy.

Each person in the relationship has the freedom to think for themselves and believes that their opinions are valued— instead of feeling pressured to agree. Together, you build an atmosphere encouraging stimulating conversation. In other words, intellectual intimacy connects your brain to that of your partner's, and gives you a shared space where you feel encouraged to voice your free thoughts and opinions.

When intellectual intimacy between your partner and you is at an optimum level, you can talk about your dreams and hopes and also feel happy when you see each other hit those checklists. Your connection becomes a fertile ground for you to find common aspirations which you can work on together while also maintaining separate interests.

Although your opinions may differ on different topics— from finances, politics, food to parenting and relationships, you always feel free to share your notions without worrying about being judged. You also become intimately aware of each other's fears, challenging past experiences, and thought patterns that are the most difficult to face. As you walk through life's hurdles and good times together, both of you help each other deal with the hardships and derive protection from simply being a team.

Intellectual intimacy is beautiful for so many reasons, but most of all because it gives you a space where you can talk about pretty much anything and at any time. If they are busy or need a few moments of quietness, they will always respectfully say they'll get back to you once their work or other commitment is complete. When you're talking, you do more than just blurt out words. You converse about the things that matter and the things that are so silly but precious, like how salt can make ice cream flavors pop, to why anti-vaccine is still a thing.

Examples Of Intellectual Intimacy

- Partners debate the importance of a college education without feeling the need to be "right." They just enjoy hearing the other person's rationale.

- A couple disagrees about which actor played the best Joker. Each person understands their theory is strictly opinion-based and enjoys the back-and-forth.

- Spouses discuss the purpose of existence. They don't believe there's a concrete answer to the question,

"What's the meaning of life?" Each entertains ideas they may not have considered otherwise.

- A couple reads and discusses a book together. The two are eager to compare their takeaways instead of arguing about why their summation of the plotline makes more sense.

How To Increase Intellectual Intimacy

Begin by being interested in what your partner has to say about different topics outside of your immediate relationship. Build a safe space where they feel comfortable, and even excited sharing their opinions about a range of topics on things they like. For instance, if they are fond of wildlife, watch a few documentaries and engage in a discussion with them. You'll be surprised at how much you learn in the process. On a deeper level, also allow them to work through past insecurities with you.

Take time to learn new skills with each other. Of course both of you should have different interests, but that doesn't mean you can't share anything. Find hobbies that stimulate both of you— even if it's just watching a mysterious whodunit on Friday nights and then discussing why someone other than the killer felt like the likelier suspect— and commit to making a routine out of these hobbies. Don't shy away from the word "routine" thinking it'll make life boring. In reality, it will give you comfort and excitement within the boundaries of doing something that brings you and your partner closer to each other.

Plan trips together. Visiting new places, experiencing different cultures and how people live, partaking in local traditions and enjoying local cuisine can bring both of you closer to each other. Plus, planning and executing trips is a great way to understand how both of you solve problems and think, as well as how you function as a team.

Share core values. Spend time understanding and appreciating how your partner looks at the world. If you spend the entire relationship constantly attacking the other person's point of view, it will become exhausting after a period. Instead, seek commonalities and learn to be inspired by their outlook. Be upfront about your personal values and where you draw your boundaries. The more they respect these values, the more you know you have found a keeper.

Experiential Intimacy

Perhaps you're confused about what exactly constitutes experiencing intimacy in comparison to other forms of closeness. Spending all of your time together as a pair is not required. However, it is essential that the two of you set aside some time to connect with one another and learn from one another's experiences. Sharing your daily lives and being close is at the heart of experiential intimacy.

Experiential intimacy refers to a type of closeness based on shared experiences. Little conversation is spoken during these intimate moments; instead, the focus is on fully immersed in the task at hand and experiencing a deep sense of closeness. Shared experiences lead to inside jokes and private memories that can intensify a connection. The act of teamwork and moving in unison toward a common goal while creating an experience also establishes a feeling of closeness. This bond is the result of experiential intimacy.

Examples Of Experiential Intimacy

- A couple trains and runs a marathon together. This allows them to support and push each other toward a confidence-building achievement.

- Partners cook a joint meal. One prepares the entrée, and the other makes dessert or side dishes to help foster teamwork.

A couple goes for an extended bike ride. Someone is responsible for planning the route while the other pack snacks and water.

- Two lovebirds visit a city neither person has been to before so that both will discover it for the first time together.

How To Increase Experiential Intimacy

Engage in a manner of new shared experiences with your companion to deepen your connection. The two of you should accomplish something that you haven't done before. You may also make the same restaurant your regular meeting place by setting up a recurring date there. A couple doesn't have to be together all the time. Sharing experiences is more important than collaborating on everything. In this manner, your shared experiences and expertise become a part of your intimate connection.

Building experiential intimacy is all about trying to increase and enjoy the mutual experiences in a relationship. You need to be *intentional* about what you are doing. So, don't ask your partner to do something with a negative connotation. For instance, don't begin a conversation by sharing something by saying, "I know you hate going on walks, but would you like to come along anyway?" Here, you are actively giving them the chance to bail out.

What would you do if you were invited to experience something by your partner, with the full disclaimer that you can say no if you hate partaking in this experience? There is such a high chance they would refuse or say something on the lines of waiting for you when you come home. The key is to approach the topic a little differently. Say something like, "let's talk about *(add shared interest or curiosity here)* on a walk together."

Spiritual Intimacy

Physical intimacy connects two bodies as one. Emotional intimacy bridges the gap between two hearts, and intellectual intimacy links minds. Spiritual intimacy occurs when your soul, the deepest aspect of your inner being, is attuned to that of your partner's. Do not make the quick judgment of thinking this has to include a religious aspect— for your spirit and religious values need not be one and the same. If you two find faith in shared religious experiences, it supplements and compliments spiritual intimacy, but is not necessary for it. The spirit is the source of your Being and your self-awareness of it. It is this common acknowledgment of the inherent awareness that forms the core of spiritual intimacy.

Spiritual intimacy ripens when you are able to discover life's transient and deep questions together. You explore different nuances to the all-encompassing understanding of who you are, both in relation to your own self and the rest of the world. While you dream of a shared future, both of you together look to understand what the present and the future will contribute to your understanding of your individual and synergetic purposes in life.

Examples Of Spiritual Intimacy

- Partners watch the sunrise (or set) together, marveling at the phenomenon.

- A couple takes a walk through the park while holding hands, enjoying the beauty of nature and each other's company.

- Spouses connect as they stand in quiet awe, overlooking the Grand Canyon.

- Partners discuss their ethics and personal definitions of spirituality. The discussion deepens their understanding of each other.

- A couple reads a few passages from their religious text before bed every night. Doing so helps them relax and feel mutually attuned with a power greater than themselves.

How To Increase Spiritual Intimacy

The first step to connecting spiritually with a loved one is to understand yourself inside out. Develop a deep knowledge of your values and beliefs. Repeatedly ask yourself the rationale and emotions behind what you believe in and what you'd like your partner to value as well. Before you connect with someone else, you need to have a complete sense of connection with your inner self.

Do not carry any toxicity of your past relationships or the marriage that has failed you. Holding on to the bad memories will only culminate in resentment and bitterness. Carry the good learnings and the beautiful shared experiences. But let the negatives go, one slow step at a time. Begin with a blank slate so you can foster new understanding with your partner.

Commit to something deeper and more pervasive than the transient physicality of the human body. The innovative notion that your purpose is to assist each other on your road to ultimate growth, to become your greatest self, is what lifts a spiritual partnership over and above an ordinary relationship. This is because your role is to help each other become your best self. Make it obvious that you are searching for opportunities to develop your spirituality in addition to finding emotional and physical support. This indicates that you are assisting one another on your journey to become a being that is more enlightened.

Finally, make spirituality a component part of your relationship. If you and your spouse are arguing with each other or if you are going through a difficult time in general, you might find solace in your spiritual practice. Give your partner permission to join you in participating in this comfortable activity with you. If you and your significant other are at a loss for how to resolve a situation, look to your faith for guidance. Permit your spiritual convictions to serve as the guiding force in your relationship. Allow the decisions you make with your spouse to be guided by the beliefs you both hold in common.

Building a spiritual connection with your partner will be one of the most enjoyable and rewarding things you do. It will feel that the relationship is right *for the right reasons*. With focused intention, you will have built something for the ages.

There are four different kinds of relationships that you may have with the same person, and each of these non-physical forms of intimacy contributes to them. Relationships that are healthy involve relating to one another on other levels in addition to the physical one. The intangible feeling of closeness that will help build your love life may be established more easily with the help of learning to engage in open and honest communication as well as working to better understand your partner.

7 Key Factors Within Any Intimate Relationship

All of us are looking out for ways to make our relationships exciting. We desire different forms of intimacy that will fulfill us in more ways than one. While every relationship is different, certain commonalities lay the groundwork for harmony in each one. If these are ignored or misused, there can be complications. Let us break down each of the key factors that you need in your relationship.

- Trust: You need to be able to share the most personal parts of yourself, including your deepest worries, fears, and insecurities. When you trust your partner, you not only feel safe in their presence, you're also content when they are busy at work or are attending an event where you aren't present.

- Acceptance: You know you've established some intimacy when you feel like a person accepts you for who you truly are. You are free to just be your authentic self. When you first meet someone, you might worry they'll hear your guilty pleasure music playlist and think you're weird. But as authentic intimacy grows between you two, you can rock out to your favorite boy bands and trust that no matter how weird you get, you'll still be accepted and cared for.

- Authenticity: Authenticity and intimacy feed one other. You often can't have one without the other. You feel comfortable telling your partner exactly how you feel because you've become so close. And in the same vein, every time you open up, you can grow a little closer. You'll know your partner is willing to listen the next time you want to share something personal.

- Safety: Sharing your deepest, truest self with another person can put you in a vulnerable place. That's why you tend to guard up when you meet someone new. You don't yet know if they'll support you as you are. But the more intimate you become, the more you'll feel you unsheathe all your vulnerabilities around them with no fear of rejection.

- Compassion: You need your people, it's as simple as that. You need love and validation after facing something tough. And while many of us feel guilty for holding these expectations, they are completely natural in all relationships— even healthy. Your partner should be your shoulder whenever storms hit, just as much as your cheerleader when you are in high spirits. Make it a point to include a daily ritual that the two of you share in your normal routine. This might entail anything from sharing a cup of morning coffee before heading off to work to reading a book together before turning in for the night.

- Affection: The world is full of non-verbal communication. Most of the time, all we want to do is be in the company of the people we care about the most. Even the smallest of nonverbal behaviors may make a world of difference when you notice your spouse going through a difficult period and you are unsure how your words might aid them. Give them a hug. Make them a cup of their favorite beverage. Order a nice meal and share it with them. In whatever ways

- Communication: There's a reason good communication is so often named the key to a healthy relationship. When you make an effort to listen to someone and tell them how you feel, you can build a deep understanding of each other. And the more you understand each other, the closer you become.

The important qualities you share as a couple must be built over time. You won't wake up one morning and say, "We're intimate now. Mission accomplished!" Intimacy is quality that you continue to cultivate over time— and that's partly why it is so beautiful. It can never diminish, only grow— so long as you remain committed to each other. The more time you spend sharing experiences and feelings, the more you build intimacy.

Naturally, it doesn't always come easy. You might feel some apprehension or even fear at the onset. That's understandable, considering that intimacy requires you to be vulnerable and put faith in other people when there's a chance they'll let you down. If anyone has ever violated your trust, it can take a while to want to take a chance once again.

So, why risk intimacy if there's a chance of getting hurt? Well, intimacy comes with health benefits that you simply can't get any other way. Deep companionship helps combat loneliness and feelings of isolation which can contribute to serious depression and mental anxiety. Intimacy boosts serotonin and reduces stress levels.

Feel-good hormones are awakened from touches like hugs and emotional releases like sharing a moment of levity with your partner. Intimacy can strengthen your immune system, lower blood pressure, and reduce your risk for heart disease. In essence, it is a key building block for a happy, healthy, and fulfilling life.

What To Do About The Fear Of Intimacy

Intimacy avoidance or avoidance anxiety stems from a fear of sharing close relationships. Most of us who go through these issues don't really *wish* to shun intimacy— as a matter of fact, we may even long for closeness, but we push others away because of our deep-seated anxieties. Several causes contribute to this avoidance, including a history of troubled childhood experiences, repeated failed relationships in the past, and going through neglect and abuse. Overcoming the anxiousness can take time. Keep exploring and understanding contributing issues and slowly ease into being vulnerable in front of your partner.

Begin by consciously identifying and naming the origins. Your fear of intimacy may be obvious to you, but it's also possible to be afraid of intimacy without even realizing it. You might avoid deep relationships or feel anxious about social situations for unclear reasons. Consider if you isolate yourself from other people, have low self-esteem or experience a hard time staying present during sex. Do you feel letting people get to know you is going to come back to bite you? These are all telltale signs.

Once you know your patterns, trace them to their roots. Find out what it was about your past relationships, whether with your families or your previous marriage, that gave birth to these anxieties. Did you feel rejected by them? Or were you always privy to destructive interactions? Does it feel like the negative dynamics you've experienced in your previous relationships can harm you even now?

For instance, it would be understandable for a person to develop a fear of intimacy as a response to a traumatic experience such as sexual assault or childhood neglect. After surviving mistreatment, we may feel the need to isolate ourselves from the rest of the world in order to protect ourselves from more condemnation and pain. After you've identified what makes you feel safe and what causes your anxiety, you can now set the boundaries that you want to maintain and begin to distance yourself from the ones that aren't serving you anymore. Once you've done this, you'll be in a better position to face your fears.

If we are unable to differentiate between positive and negative or self-limiting adaptive responses to our past experiences, it will be incredibly hard for us to live our own existence as happy, individualistic adults, and it will be even more difficult to partake in long-term romantic relationships. One of the most helpful activities we can do to improve our love lives is to place our feelings and perceptions back where they belong. As we begin to appreciate how our past informs our present, we may decide to cease seeing our spouse in a suspicious or rejecting light. And this will be the onset of your journey into intimacy.

Communicate your feelings. It is difficult to establish trust with someone who is unaware that you are going through a challenging time in your life. If you have a love relationship, you should let them know that it is difficult for you to let go of control and that you are working on overcoming this challenge. You ought to be able to open up about what you're frightened of and the origins of those worries. It is perfectly acceptable and in fact, I would argue that it is extremely vital, to articulate to the people in your life what it is that you need from them to feel secure within your relationships.

Make it a point to convey your appreciation for your partner. Show your gratitude, which can take the form of gifts, favors, or a simple "thank you." You will find there is always something beautiful to learn about them. I have acquired so much knowledge of native American history simply by enquiring about the backgrounds of my close circle— their families, their ancestors, and the stories they carry. Human beings are vessels of different happenings, both internal and external to them. Use every opportunity you get to learn more about your partner and their history.

Plan a weekly date night, a monthly board game night, or a nightly moment to check in a one-on-one before bedtime, away from the kids or other responsibilities. During this time, unplug and focus on each other without any electronics getting in the way. Spending time together without electronics can give you a chance to give each other some undivided attention.

Show physical affection (even without sex). If you have a sexual relationship, then mixing things up with new toys, outfits, and fantasies can keep things interesting. But you can also build intimacy by making it a point to show physical affection without sex. Share plenty of warm gestures and cuddles. Hold each other's hands when you have deep conversations. Hug each other at the end of those yucky fights. After all, joining your bodies together is about more than just "getting off."

Tackle a project together. Restore a piece of furniture, learn a new skill like baking, or teach your old dog some new tricks. Whatever the project, working toward a goal with a loved one can cultivate bonding time, make invaluable memories, and give you something new to look forward to in the presence of each other's company.

Talk about what intimacy means to you. Building intimacy doesn't have to be a guessing game. An easy way to figure out how to build closeness is to just talk about it! Tell your loved one how you'd like to spend time together and what activities help you feel more connected to them. Then listen when they tell you their version— and narrow down on some things you can begin as soon as possible.

Chapter 9

Effective Communication

Imagine this. You come home after a long day of work. Your partner had asked you to return a little early because they had something special planned for you. But things flew out of your control, and before you know it, the clock shows it's eleven pm the moment you set foot inside your house. Your partner is waiting in the dining room. When you see them, all you say is, "I'm sorry, love. It's been a difficult day at work." They respond with, "Go change, let's have dinner and we'll talk about it."

Now, imagine an alternate scenario. You set foot inside the house. The minute your partner sees you, instead of giving you any room to talk, they begin shouting. "How dare you come home so late? You've ruined everything! I had so much planned and now it's all cold and stale. Why do you even bother?"

Which scenario would you rather have going for you?

Communicating in relationships is essential to having a happy, healthy partnership. Your partner is likely the person you spend the most time with, which means there's a greater risk of misunderstandings and conflict. But when you perfect communication in relationships, you'll be rewarded. You've had your fair share of tense moments if you're in a relationship. It's OK to have arguments — clashing is a normal part of being a couple.

Communication Builds Both Parties In A Relationship

A partner who doesn't interact with you isn't letting you in on a significant part of who they are. They do this for a variety of reasons, but they keep their emotions and ideas bottled up within. Fear of being rejected and worry that they may say or do something to make their partner sad are two reasons why individuals in relationships often struggle to communicate effectively. Even if the latter emotion is important, failing to communicate with your spouse about what you need prevents the connection from evolving and developing. If you want your relationship to last a long time and provide you satisfaction, then growth is very necessary.

Developing a stronger and more intimate bond is essential to the success of any long-term relationship. These strategies may help you enhance your immune system, regardless of how long you've been together or how recently you started dating your significant other. According to studies on the factors that contribute to the success of marriages, happy and healthy couples have a positive behavior to negative behavior ratio of five to one in their relationships. This means there are five times as many positive interactions between happy couples (i.e., listening, validating the other person, using soft words, expressing appreciation, affirmation, physical affection, compliments, etc.) as there are negative (i.e., raising one's voice, incessantly complaining, or expressing anger).

Communication Helps You Grow Together

A few years back, I was stuck in the lowest phase of my life. My last relationship had ended a while before, but I wasn't ready to accept it. I felt there was no one else out there in the world for me— not only because I was unworthy, but because the whole process of opening up to someone again, going through the same motions, recounting all my experiences— all of it felt so tiresome. I was essentially done.

It took me a long time to get my emotions to a stable place, but even after that, I was determined to not waste time on love. Then, someone came into my life when I wasn't looking for anything more than a good friend. And for a while there, that's all we were. What struck me the most was how easy it was for me to communicate with them. It didn't feel like a tedious task or something I'd hate doing. I found myself looking forward to the moments we'd spend, discussing all the big and little things. In the end, it wasn't about who I chose.

What was much more important was that they gave me a home where I felt safe, nurtured, and capable of experiencing growth. Real communication in romantic partnerships necessitates an openness to discuss everything with one's partner, including happy and sad times, as well as both good and negative news. You are willing to put yourself in a vulnerable position with them because you are certain that they will love and support you no matter what.

Additionally, communication will help you sail through those discussions which aren't as easy. We've all seen couples that seem to argue often, as well as those who never seem to have any problems. Though every relationship goes through rough patches, both constant bickering and a complete absence of conflict are symptoms of a communication breakdown. The key is not to avoid disagreements but to become better at conflict resolution.

Learning how to communicate better in relationships is a great way to deepen your emotional connection with your significant other. Improving your communication abilities demonstrates that you value and respect your conversational partner's thoughts and feelings. Closeness on a deeper, more emotional level, and even physical intimacy, may blossom when two individuals are treated with respect and acceptance.

Is There Such A Thing As Over-Communication?

Yes, there are situations in which there is too much communication in a relationship. When people are anxious or unsure about how to express themselves, they often resort to one of two typical defense mechanisms: internalizing or externalizing. When faced with conflict, those who internalize tend to shut down and retreat, while those who externalize want to talk it out, often to an unhealthy extreme.

More talking doesn't always mean better talking. Some people need time alone to gather their thoughts before speaking, while others need to slow down and hone their message. While it's true that talking things out may fix a lot of issues in a relationship, it's also possible to communicate too much. Specifically, an abundance of negative discourse. It's not always important to let your spouse know exactly what's going on in your head. While it's normal to be upset with your spouse from time to time, it's not productive to constantly bring up your issues. Your spouse may feel attacked and knit picked if you keep pointing out what's going wrong in the relationship and why you are always stressing out over it.

So, the context of over-communication will depend on the kind of relationship you are in. If you gravitate towards needing conflict resolutions quickly, and your partner wants to take their time to process their feelings, you may risk saying too much. To prevent that, consider slowing down and processing your message in terms of what you know about your partner before you go too deep into elaborations.

How To Communicate

Good communication can be the difference between a strong, lifelong partnership or a conflict-filled bond that culminates in disappointment. Learning how to communicate better is vital.

Commit To Developing True Connection

The biggest misconception about communicating in a relationship is that communication works the same way as talking or making conversation. Communication in relationships, at its core, is about connecting and using your verbal, written, and physical skills to fulfill your partner's needs. You can even communicate with so much as your eyes or hands, and nothing else. It's not about making small talk or asking about the weather. When communication is good, your partner will understand your pain and joy without you needing to recount explicitly how you feel in words. It's about understanding your partner's point of view, offering support, and letting your partner know you are their #1 fan.

It's easy to let real connection and passion diminish, especially in long-term relationships. But the first key to improving communication in a relationship is to realize you're not connecting the way you used to. Talk with your partner about rekindling your connection and provide a starting point. If your partner isn't on board, don't worry. Relationships are where you go to give, not where you go to take. You can still enact many of these strategies without a commitment from your partner – and you may even inspire them to reciprocate.

Identify Communication Styles

Before you work on learning how to improve communication in a relationship, you need to realize that not everyone has the same communication style. The four main communication styles are passive, aggressive, passive-aggressive, and assertive. Passive communicators keep their emotions inside and are the ones who can never seem to refuse anything, therefore they run the risk of getting manipulated and abused. Aggressive communicators are loud and intense but typically have trouble making real connections with others. Passive-aggressive communicators avoid conflict and use sarcasm to deflect real communication. The healthiest type of communication comes from those who are assertive. These people are in touch with their emotions and know how to communicate them effectively.

Communication styles also include our metaprograms, which refer to the way in which we react to information. Some individuals prefer to engage in verbal exchanges, while others are more intuitive or find that receiving a present is a more satisfactory expression of their emotions than expressing themselves verbally. You are well aware of the kind of communication that best suits you, but is this also the case with your partner?

Relationships and methods of interaction vary greatly. Recognizing this will help you and your spouse improve your communication.

If you want to improve your communication skills, try observing your partner's reactions to a variety of subtle hints over the course of a couple of days. Do they seem to react more to what they see and hear? Listening and conversing? A combination of the two, perhaps? For instance, if your partner is more attuned to audible cues such as language and tone, your efforts to make frequent eye contact and use soft facial expressions may not be as effective as you believe. No matter how many signals you send, no one seems to be responding to them. On the other end, saying "I love you" may not be enough if, for example, you are an auditory person, and your partner is a kinesthetic person who enjoys the sensation of touch. Remember to reinforce your affection with physical contact as much as possible.

Discover The Six Human Needs

There are six fundamental needs that all humans share, but each of us places these needs in a different order depending on our core values. Once you discover which needs matter the most to your partner, you'll know how to communicate with your partner in a way that fulfills them.

The first human need is for certainty. This need drives us to seek out pleasure and avoid pain, stress, and emotional risks. Ask yourself these questions: How secure is my partner feeling in our relationship? We all find safety and comfort in different things. Be open with your partner about what gives them certainty and makes them feel stable.

The next need affecting communication and relationships is the need for variety. Uncertainty isn't always scary if you know how to communicate with your partner. Relationships need healthy challenges that allow partners to grow together. As you learn to communicate better, variety keeps things fun and exciting with your partner.

Significance is the third human need. We all need to feel unique and important. Communication is key to this desire because your partner needs to know that you singularly need them – that they fulfill your needs in ways that only they can. How do you demonstrate to your partner, not just tell them, that they are significant to you? You can show them through loving touch, offering them support when needed, and spending quality time with them.

Fourth, you need connection and love. Every human being has a natural tendency to seek out connections. We all want to be understood and appreciated for who we are. Effective communication in relationships lets us know that we are loved and can make us feel at our most alive, but the absence of love can cause pain and emptiness. Too often, we automatically say "I love you" to solve a conflict with our partners and forget to show love in a real, tangible way that speaks to our partner's needs. Reverse this pattern: consciously show your partner that you love them every day in a way that speaks to their personal preferences and needs.

Learning how to improve communication in a relationship is about realizing what "language" your partner best understands and giving them love that mirrors this language. Food is my love language, and my partner intrinsically understands this. Every time I come back home on a day when my mood isn't the best, there's a hot, nourishing, home-cooked meal waiting for me at the dining table. That tells me my partner loves me more than anything else could.

Growth is the fifth human need. The ultimate human experience is one of motion, and without constant growth, our relationships will become stale. We constantly endeavor to evolve along the different paths that interest us the most, whether these are emotional, intellectual, spiritual, or otherwise. Your partner needs growth as much as you, and when we learn how to communicate better, we can also learn how to grow together better.

When was the last time you supported your partner's growth in the areas that they are most passionate about? How can you continue to support them to the fullest? Think of the answers to this question. Also think if there is an area in your life where both of you can grow as a couple. Maybe you'd like to take some classes together or acquire a new skill with each other. Find out what it is and work on it as a team.

The sixth and final human need is contribution and giving. Remember, the secret to loving is giving. Contribution is our source of meaning – it determines who we become and solidifies our legacy, who we are, and our role in the world. Consider what you give to your partner and the different ways in which you can fulfill them while also maintaining healthy boundaries.

Are you giving your time? Your undivided attention when they are trying to share something that matters to them? The benefit of the doubt? A second chance if situations call for it? When communication in relationships is strong, both partners can continually develop new and better ways of contributing to the other's happiness.

Learn The Three Keys To Passion And Intimacy

The strongest relationships have polarity: opposing masculine and feminine energies complementing each other. When the needs of either person aren't being met, that person will put on a "mask" of the opposing energy and close off from their partner. But when polarity in relationships is fully embraced, a beautiful connection is created.

Masculine and feminine energies each have three key needs that must be met. Feminine energies need to feel seen— they want you to be present with and appreciate them. They need to feel understood through listening and validation. And they crave feeling safe, both physically and emotionally.

Masculine energies need to feel appreciated through praise and celebration. They want to be free from being micromanaged or controlled. And they need to feel opened up to – so share your emotions and affection freely.

Communication in relationships is about first fulfilling your partner's needs. They will be more open to communicating and connecting with you to create your desired relationship when you do that. Remember— masculine and feminine energies are not related to any specific gender. A woman can have an abundance of masculine energies inside her. She can be strongly independent and abhor being controlled or micromanaged.

In the same breath, a man can have feminine energies which means he likes being appreciated and wants to feel safe in his relationships. This is entirely dependent on how your partner navigates through the relationship you have, but it's safe to assume *all* of us have both energies in us, just in different proportions. The key to a healthy relationship is to balance the energies as properly as you can.

Determine If Your Partner's Needs Are Being Met

One surefire way to know if your partner is getting their needs met in your relationship is to ask the right questions and then deeply listen to the answers. Reflect on what your partner says, and if you're unsure what he or she means, then ask by restating their point and asking if you understand correctly.

The key to communicating in a relationship is often not in verbal communication— it's in the way we listen to our partner. Your partner will want to *see* and *feel* you have heard and understood what they are saying and where they are coming from. Words are not always the best ways of expressing your understanding. Think of what your partner likes when they are craving your presence and think of how you can fulfill their needs.

Your partner may be communicating exactly the problem, but you'll miss it if you're not listening. Resist the pull of just waiting for your partner to finish what they're saying so you can launch into your "turn." That isn't listening; it's waiting to talk. Instead, listen with a calm, open mind and hear what they are saying to you. This will help you learn how to communicate better and enable you to connect with your partner on a deeper level.

Be Honest And Open

Honesty will help even the hardest of relationships thrive, so long as both partners are absolutely clear on their comforts and needs. Say what you mean, and make your feelings and requirements clear. Retreating from conflict seems deceptively safe and comfortable, but it's no substitute for trust in a relationship, and it will never help you learn how to communicate better. Walking away from an argument is a temporary way to deal with an ongoing communication issue and must only be done to achieve a brief cooling-down period. When you disagree with your partner, you must trust that what you say will be heard and respected, and so does your partner.

If you or your partner (or both of you) are averse to conflict, you can find yourselves burying your emotions to please each other and avoid problems. This temporary peacekeeping band-aid turns a two-way relationship into a one-directional affair where one or both parties are bound to get hurt— which is not a sustainable outcome. The happiness and intimacy you used to share will gradually erode, and it will take the relationship with it. Instead of ignoring issues, you both must learn how to communicate better.

Be Present In The Moment

Imagine you are sharing something important with your partner. You finish saying what you have going on in your mind, then ask them for their opinion. They respond with a blank stare. You ask once again, and they say, "I'm sorry, could you repeat that once again? I blanked out." Now imagine this happening every other day. Wouldn't it be frustrating? In any relationship, being present to listen to and take care of your partner is essential.

Put some time aside everyday where you dedicate yourself 100% to communicating with your partner. They must truly feel that they have your full attention and that they are your number one priority.

It's difficult to listen and be fully present, aware, and mindful when you're angry and stressed or are working on things that take time away from your relationship. This is a part of life, but it's important to realize that it's not an excuse for neglecting communication in relationships. Remember that intimacy, love, and trust are built when times are hard, not easy. If we gave up at every sign of resistance, we would never progress and evolve. Seize these opportunities to learn how to deal with conflict and stress healthily and watch as you grow and flourish with your partner.

Let Petty Conflicts Go

You will fight. That's an inevitability. But choose your battles wisely, because if you fight over every tiny issue, the relationship will become more about keeping score than working as a team. When you do have disagreements, don't always bring up mistakes your partner may have made in the past, or things their family may have said. Don't go down the line of, "your mother/father/sibling said so and so..." Instead, focus on what the disagreement means for you right now, and how you can best solve it.

Resist letting a discussion about what's happening now devolve into a rehash of every wrong that has ever happened between you and your partner. This is the opposite of loving and effective communication in relationships. Instead, assess the present situation and identify what you can do at this moment.

Pause and remember why you're here, and remember that your goal, the outcome that you value, is to strengthen your relationship, build intimacy and learn how to communicate better. There's absolutely nothing you can do about the past right now, so let it go.

Learning the tools of communication is about more than saying the right things. Also, be aware of your body language. You could offer your partner all the loving and supportive words, but if your arms are crossed over your chest, and you have a scowl on your face, your partner will not respond favorably. Communicating in a relationship means listening, loving, and supporting with your whole being. Lean toward your partner, keep your face relaxed and open and gently touch them. Show them through all your words, actions, and expressions that you love them even if you are in conflict.

Break Negative Patterns

You know what your partner needs. You've thought about their preferred communication style. Yet, something is still missing. Well, there is another thing affecting communication in relationships: how you speak. Communication experts break down how we talk into pitch, pace, volume, and timbre. The next time you're in a disagreement with your partner, be mindful and make conscious efforts to modulate these aspects of your voice.

An overly high-pitched voice sounds defensive and immature. Also, if you end a sentence with a higher pitch, it sounds like a question; don't do this unless you're asking a question, or you risk instilling doubt in your partner.

Pacing is symbolic of how fast you're talking. Take a deep breath and slow down –especially when you're disagreeing. Speak calmly and clearly to get your message across.

Pay attention to volume, especially volume "creep," and avoid shouting because you feel what you are saying is more important. Being louder won't help you communicate with your partner. If your partner is speaking, listen.

Timbre refers to your voice's emotional quality, attitude, and tone. Pay careful attention to this, and watch for red flag timbres like sarcasm that can erode communication in relationships and cause distrust between partners.

When things do get out of hand, break the pattern: if the situation warrants it, be playful and use humor to keep the conversation flowing in the right direction. Injecting humor into the situation can make it feel less dire and yield amazing results for a couple. Humor helps you regain perspective and balance; it is an essential component of healthy communication in relationships. It also relieves stress and improves your physical happiness in your everyday life.

The biggest benefit to laughing in this context is that it reminds you that you love just being together with your partner. It reminds you that you can enjoy your time together, even when things seem challenging. Plus, it's a sign you are willing to talk things out. Again, don't use sarcastic or demeaning humor to put your partner down. Always remember this is someone you love and want to keep around.

When learning how to communicate in a relationship, it's important to break the hostility, hurt, and retreat pattern. For example, change your tone when you catch yourself raising your voice or being sarcastic. If you're using "you" repeatedly and blaming your partner, switch to "I" and "me," or better yet, "we." There's no point in offloading all your relationship issues to your partner. There are two people in every relationship, so consider what you can do to solve your issues together, not separately.

Breaking the pattern is a powerful way of reframing the discussion and bringing it back to a level where you can get to what matters. Communication in relationships is all about what your partner's needs are, what your needs are, and how you can both feel fulfilled from your relationship.

Start Over

Sometimes no matter how much you want to improve communication in a relationship, an argument happens. This is when it's essential to be aware of your negative patterns and not let them reach destructive heights.

If you were born before the mid-80s, you should remember the Cold War. It was a defining period of world history when two superpowers with opposite ideologies – i.e., differences in values— confronted each other in a tense political conflict that could, at any point, tip toward a crushing nuclear war. It was not a productive relationship, and in the late-80s, the leaders of the two powers met in a series of talks that would forever shape the course of human history.

But, the story of how Reagan, president of the United States, and Gorbachev, leader of the Soviet Union, resolved the conflict did not start as well as you might think. Gorbachev and Reagan found themselves in the middle of a heated discussion on the merits and demerits of capitalism and communism. Like any discussion on politics, it was going nowhere and neither leader was sure how to communicate better with the other.

Then, in the middle of the argument, Reagan stood and walked away, only to suddenly turn and exclaim, "OK, let's try this again. I'm Ronald!" If Reagan and Gorbachev can start over after so much bitterness, there's hope for communication in your relationship.

Always remember that you are together because you make each other smile. Problems are obstacles that need surmounting, and while it's easy to give up, the truth is that these are the moments that will define your relationship. Listen to your partner, discover the needs they value the most, and fulfill them. When you understand that giving is the secret to a fulfilling relationship, you'll put constant work into how to communicate with your partner in a way they can understand.

Chapter 10

State Your Needs And Intentions

A year into her divorce, Martha wakes up one morning feeling she is ready for a change. She has taken three hundred and sixty-five days to heal and work on herself. On this day, she intends to find a healthy relationship that will fulfill her emotionally, spiritually, and physically. Now, Martha could go one of two ways. She could immediately join an online hookup forum and fall for someone incredibly charming.

Her reasoning would be— "oh, okay, I know he doesn't fit my dreams, but I'll look for someone stable later." Or, she could translate her thoughts and desires into real action, where she meets people, but waits for the man who makes her feel what she wants. If she goes the first route, she's just stuck on the plane of wanting something. She may never achieve it. If she goes the second route, she is setting intentions for what she wants and will likely achieve it.

Simply speaking, an intention is focusing on a specific direction that you hope things will go. That can happen with your goals for the new year, and you can also have intentions in a relationship. The intention setting is clearly elucidating what you want to achieve with your actions.

Love intentions are not as much about planning but more about a divine concentration that's more of the heart than of mind. A person can have good intentions if they're looking for a positive connection.

In that case, they will share only the healthiest aspects of a partnership with a compatible partner. It's up to a prospective partner to realize whether those intentions are authentic.

How Do You Know Your Intentions?

Intentions in a relationship are something you either feel committed to within your heart and soul or don't. When you're with someone, your instincts will kick in, and you'll know if there's a connection. It may not even be romantic right at the onset, but it *must* feel as if the person you are speaking to is someone who empathizes with and understands you.

Knowing you are in a safe space will slowly develop intentions for your blossoming relationship. You will see whether you'd like to move forward or if you want to wait for someone different. You will also know whether you intend to be an open book— that is, if it is completely okay for you to be vulnerable and lay all your cards out right at the onset or take things a little slow.

A more realistic question is how to know your partner's intentions, which takes time. They can express them to you and will when prodded, but actions speak louder than words. As you spend more time with them, measure their authenticity. Do they show up when they say they will? Can they read between the lines? Are they kind to those around them?

The idea of intentions is to commit to bringing specific components to a partnership in hopes that it can move forward healthfully. When one person sets intentions, they should be able to hope that the other person has comparable commitments for the relationship. If you intend to have a romantic, long-lasting relationship with the person you are dating, but they intend for a casual fling, there will be conflict.

When you want to move forward in a relationship where you have deep feelings for someone and things are frustratingly stuck in one place, it's wise to reevaluate each person's intentions for the future.

What Do Intentions Mean?

True intentions in a relationship are not necessarily goals since these are reserved for general life circumstances but rather hopes, anticipations, and perhaps a dream that you foresee as the partnership progresses.

Once you determine that a partner is someone you want to move forward with more exclusively, there comes the point where you need to discuss your intentions with this relationship to see where each of you stand.

First and foremost, there needs to be a specific level of self-love intentions before you can love someone else freely and fully with intention.

Ensuring that you are strong in confidence, individuality, and independence allows you to share with another person but not depend on someone else. The expectation in return for love with intention should be comparable.

What Are Good Intentions?

Good intentions for dating are specific positive accomplishments that you commit to yourself and your partner to achieve for that partnership as it progresses. They are the little things you simply want to do for your partner or wish for them to have because you care deeply about them.

A union can only be healthy when two people work at it. It takes considerable effort in the beginning and throughout your lifetime to retain that passion, grow that love and respect, and establish a closeness that will endure age and life's numerous stresses. Here are some good intentions you could have for your relationship:

- I will show kindness and respect to my partner.

- Every day, good or bad, I will seek to complement my partner and work as a team to resolve our issues.

- I will always be genuine in my relationship with my partner.

- When I feel I am being neglected, I will talk it out with my partner and come to an agreement without belittling him.

- I will always look for the good things in my partner and be committed to being deeply in love with them.

How Do Couples Set Intentions?

Dating with intention can be challenging, but there are ways you can set intentions in how you present yourself to the people you care about. I've narrowed down on some tips that will help you do this.

10 Tips On How To Set Intentions

Things are constantly changing on a daily basis; life is becoming more and more difficult every day. Amid everything, a wholesome relationship can give you strength and hope to face the world fearlessly.

You can overcome a lot of life challenges when you are naturally happy from the inside. Genuine happiness has become rare in our modern society; but it can be something you enjoy. Once you build that spark in your love life, you will find your comfort against the storm of everyday struggles.

Intentions aren't things you plan or "schedule," as we necessarily see it. These should be part of who you are. So let's look at a few rules as to how you can date with intention.

Don't compromise on your standards.

If you have friends or family members tell you that you're filtering too much, you need to let go of a few characteristics that you're looking for – no, you don't. Don't fall for that "you can't get everything you are looking for" talk.

That person with those specific traits is out there. Your search can go on as long as necessary until you find someone who meets your needs. If you settle for someone who doesn't quite add up to your expectations, you will always feel a bit hollow for what could have been.

Date with that purpose and don't compromise. Hopefully, you can progress forward with ideal intentions in a relationship if you and your partner decide to move things ahead.

Expression is key when dating initially

Many people, upon meeting, tend to put on airs instead of presenting themselves authentically. Instead of paying attention to what's happening and genuinely listening to the other person, they're busy ensuring their act is perfected throughout the date. Look at it this way. The more artificial you are, the more trouble you will have in keeping up appearances. And it won't make you happy because you are constantly under pressure to be someone *you are not.*

It should be a sincere intention to avoid this habit. Instead, present authentically so your partner can find out instantly if they feel a real sense of connection with the true you. You don't want a long-term relationship where every day becomes an examination of how good you are at acting a role. Instead, just be who you are; if they like you, they're worth it.

Lead with confidence

Set the intention to lead into the relationship feeling secure in the gifts you bring from within. Assure that you know you have an understood intention from your partner. They should know you are confident, self-assured, and independent. In the same breath, they should also compliment these characteristics.

When you have this sense of the strength of conviction, it allows your partner to present comparable strength exposing their attributes and what they intend to bring to the partnership. They won't feel the need to pretend or give an unauthentic expression of their inner selves because they will understand you are someone real in a world where so much is already filtered to look good.

Keep things smooth

The intentions in a relationship are that there should be no struggle. The suggestion here is when you consider each relationship in your life, do you find you're always tolerating or enduring hassles or difficulties? This is not the same as having disagreements. All healthy relationships have their share of challenges, but the unhealthy ones leave little to zero room for equal resolution. One party is always sacrificing more to keep the other happy.

Why would you want to do so with the person you might be spending most of your time with? No one wants that, and the idea is that it won't be happening.

A healthy relationship should be easy, smooth, and carefree. That's not saying there will never be challenges or difficulties. That's, of course, part of having a passionate, long-term partnership. Life will happen, but struggling with each other as a couple should not.

Mistakes are impossible

There are no mistakes when you're in a loving couplehood, and the intentions in a relationship mean that you never criticize or hold each other responsible for making mistakes. This is not to say there are no errors. It only means when things go wrong, you don't blame each other and instead look for healthy ways to find solutions together.

Errors are communicated, worked through, apologized for, and forgiven. Both of you understand a healthy partnership will materialize when you solve things with each other instead of continuously arguing about how imperfect you are as a couple or brushing things under the carpet. Once situations get better, you don't drag up the past whenever a problem appears. You deal with it in the present moment and trust things will improve.

Individualism is maintained and expected

When you become a couple, you don't automatically meld into one person – that is not the intention. Instead, you maintain your individuality and complement each other. You don't give up your own interests, hobbies and loves because you think it will make them love you more. Yes, compromises will sometimes be inevitable, but they should not come at the cost of you foregoing your entire identity.

The anticipation is that each person will still pursue their interests, see friends, and come together at the end of the day. Personal space is just as important as enjoying time together.

Take your intentions slowly

You shouldn't feel rushed to go toward a certain "goal" in the relationship, even if everyone's intentions are clear from the start. Before committing more time or energy, it is crucial to thoroughly understand qualities, verify that intentions are good, and determine whether or not the connection is genuine.

If you're the one feeling that things are becoming stagnant or you're finding yourself hesitating, it's wise to look at the situation again and consider whether the fit is correct, or you're having trouble breathing.

Vulnerability is a virtue

When a couple feels vulnerable, it creates a deeper link and brings them closer together. Ideally, both parties in a relationship would put out an effort to maximize this mutual benefit, which would serve to cement their bond with one another.

Suppose you want your partner to open up to you. In that case, you may need to demonstrate your understanding of their aims in the relationship by initiating deeper conversations that shed light on who you are, where you come from, and other aspects close to your heart.

Disallow rejection from your mindset

You are not to blame if a romantic encounter or relationship ends in disappointment. There are two persons involved, and they contribute to the development of the cracks that eventually lead to the collapse of the structure's foundation.

Make a promise to yourself that you will never allow yourself to feel guilty when things go wrong. Instead, realize that there will always be things that don't quite fit, but something better is just around the corner.

Grow through challenges

The goal is to find someone who will back you up no matter what, and vice versa.

Take it a step further by becoming that person for them.

Find someone who will push you to develop further by encouraging you to pursue your goals and objectives and providing you with continuous, varied challenges that make you the best version of yourself without changing your love or who you are.

The individual mirrors both your current self and the future self you want to become, inspiring you to go farther than you ever thought possible. An ideal relationship is one in which both partners feel fulfilled and happy, with the expectation that it will grow into something more.

If you and your partner appear to be on the same page but are unclear on how to get to the heart of the matter, a professional counselor might provide valuable input and lead you to a more positive place.

Chapter 11
Social Media Boundaries

Roughly three-quarters of adults in relationships use social media, but how does social media affect their associations? It's not uncommon to hear about people who meet their soulmates online these days. And it makes sense. You get to filter people within the convenience of your home until you meet someone who sounds just right— albeit on paper. So, when it comes to social media and relationships, where do you draw the line?

The Dangers Of Social Media When It Comes To Relationships

Social media boundaries in relationships are crucial to a healthy marriage or partnership. Discussing privacy constraints, when to make your relationship public via a status, and what interactions with exes are off-limits can stop an argument before it even starts. Even though it seems you've met someone who just fits, and you're all eager to take the meeting to the next level, remember you are only seeing a very limited side of them— that is, just the bit they want you to know about.

We all tend to look up our dates before meeting them simply because we want to know more about them. The truth is, even with all the information they put in front of us, there's very little we know about how they live their lives in real time.

Would you be able to trust a person with no online presence? Well, give it a thought. It's very difficult, isn't it? Social media platforms are an integral part of our lives, so much so that imagining a life outside of it sounds unrealistic. We may decide not to post anything or detach ourselves from social media, but after a while, we'll find ourselves hooked to it again.

Today, when moving out of social media is so difficult, imagine the impact it may have on our lives. The truth is social media destroys relationships beyond repair, and some couples constantly complain about it. It's so easy for people to tire out in their stable relationships because they've met someone seemingly better and "more perfect" online. Associations have become commercial, and with the rise of conveniences, there's a marked reduction in people who still believe in the sanctity of face-to-face relationships.

Not only that, social media also influences how we form, maintain, and end our relationships. Let's have a look at some of the adverse effects of social media on relationships and ensure that we safeguard ourselves from them.

Limited personal interaction

How does social media affect relationships? Well, it limits the intimacy of personal interactions.

Digital gadgets may have brought us close to each other, but it has also deeply impacted personal interactions. There are times when you're sitting next to your loved ones, but instead of having a one-on-one interaction with each other, you're busy chatting with a person sitting miles away.

You're only present in body, but your spirit is busy scrolling through the lives of celebrities and media personalities traveling the world and apparently having more fun than you. Social media is an eyewash, but it can paint a very realistic picture of suggesting everyone else has it better than you.

Such constant actions then create a barrier between the two-loved ones and push them apart from each other. So, make sure you keep your mobile phones aside when you're with your loved one. The digital platforms can wait and is surely not as important as the person present with you at that moment.

Reopens closed chapters

When you're in a relationship, you want to cherish it, make it special, and want to focus on it and nothing else. However, when suddenly you get a like or comment on an Instagram post from your ex, things change. It can also happen that your partner's picture gets liked by his ex, making you question things even though it isn't his fault.

Social media ruins relationships by impinging on your trust equation with your partner. It reopens closed chapters which should remain where they belong— the past. It makes you become the very person you swore not to be— someone who is constantly afraid your partner may be swayed to remembering their old relationships.

We can't pinpoint to one app and say it ruins relationships; in fact, it's the whole plethora of social media accounts that do it. In person, when you've cut ties with your ex, you've closed the chapter. But when you're active on social media and your ex comments on your post, or shows up to leave a random message, things can often go out of hand.

Obsession with sharing everything

Social media ruins relationships as many fail to draw the line between what and what not to share. When one spends excess time on social media, they usually get obsessed with sharing every detail of their life.

You share every tiny detail of your relationship for the world to view— all the romance and seemingly every crucial moment that is best kept private. God forbid, if things don't work out, you are left with very visual reminders that can sometimes just exacerbate the hurt.

Excessive PDA

Social media platforms can give you a very false perspective on what real relationships look like. Excessive displays of affection between famous couples who look like their chemistry are off the charts may make your own sweet romance seem lackluster in comparison. The truth is you don't know what's happening in their real lives— and whether they any of it is genuine or a way to earn more money through sponsorships. Plenty of companies promote couples who look "golden." On the other hand, social media can also make you believe any time a slight thing goes wrong, you can just walk out of the relationship. When you do make decisions, ensure your heart is in them and you are not being influenced by the filtered lives of others online.

Makes way for insecurities

All the major problems start with just small confusion or insecurity. Social media ruins relationships as it give birth to insecurities, which gradually take over. One small comment or like from someone else can lead to serious problems over the years. For instance, your partner is actively chatting or interacting with someone on a social media platform.

Over time, you may get suspicious of their relationship, but the reality might be way different from what you perceive. You judge your association with your partner simply because they're talking to someone else. In truth, if something like this makes you uncomfortable, it can speak to a real issue in your relationship.

Addiction sets in

One of the other effects of social media on relationships is the addiction you may develop with a platform. Before you know it, you are scrolling through video after video all day long, ignoring the real people around you. There are a lot of couples who often complain that their partner doesn't give them enough time as they're busy on their social media platforms. If this continues for a longer period, it can even lead to separation. Life is bigger than the pictures you see online, and it has much more meaning than cheesy captions that fuel your insecurities.

Constant comparison

Social media ruins relationships as couples may start to compare their bond with others. No two relationships are the same. Every couple has different ways of bonding and equations. They have their own ways of showing love to each other.

Just because someone on social media is going on trips with their partner every other day, you don't need to fall into the pressure of thinking this is the only way for someone to show they really love you. Unfortunately, this kind of pressure builds up over time and unconsciously, you begin judging your partner for what they can't do rather than being grateful for everything they're giving you. Naturally, this spells doom for your relationship.

High possibility of infidelity

Along with Facebook, Instagram, and Twitter, there are other platforms like Tinder. You might not get tempted by this platforms, but you can't guarantee your partner will share your nonchalance.

There is a chance that they are experimenting with these platforms and are gradually being pulled toward them. Hence, the chances of infidelity increase, and one can easily say that social networking is bad for relationships.

It's understood that imagining a life without social media platforms is impossible. However, when things are done within limits, it's harmless. Spending too much time on social media can be a sign your partner is not content with things the way they are, so watch out if this is the case.

How To Navigate Social Media Boundaries

We want your relationship to be healthy and grounded, not filtered and fake. Here are some guidelines to consider as you begin setting helpful social media boundaries in your relationship.

Be With Your Spouse More Than Your Facebook

Spending more time on your social accounts than you are with your partner is an indication something is amiss in your relationship. Do you ever find yourself engrossed in your phone instead of your partner, even when it's just the two of you on a date? Or was there ever a time you felt ignored by your phone-absorbed partner instead? A Pew Research study found that 25% of cell phone owners in a long-term relationship felt their partner was distracted by phone use while they were together.

Consider coming up with a plan to manage screen time. Social media can ruin a relationship when it becomes more important than the connection you and your partner share. If either of you is a serious social media addict, setting realistic expectations can be important.

Allow Your Partner To Be Your Friend Or Follower On Social Media

Some individuals find it challenging to let their partners follow or friend them on social media. What are the reasons you wouldn't want your partner to follow or friend you? This is a good question to ask and consider. Is there a lingering lack of trust that this illustrates?

Here's a scenario to contemplate: A friend and you decide to get lunch together. Your spouse, unbeknownst to you, is eating lunch at the same restaurant. So, if you saw your partner and their friend, would you say hello to them or ignore them? Most people would say hello. Most of them may even invite their significant other to come along. So, if you're comfortable with them joining you impromptu, why keep so much of yourself hidden from them when it comes to social media?

Tip: If you are in a committed relationship or considering going exclusive, becoming your partner's friend or follower is exercising good social etiquette.

Respect Your Partner's Privacy

The use of social media may cover a wide spectrum, from little exposure to extensive sharing of one's life. A healthy relationship requires compromise, and if one partner uses Facebook more openly than the other, it's crucial to find a middle ground.

Please consider your partner's privacy preferences before sharing personal information about your family, such as photos or identifying information. If you have kids, this is very crucial.

Some parents choose not to share baby pictures on Instagram. If you and your partner have different ideas about how much personal information should be shared about your kids, it's important to talk about it.

It's important to give some thought to what you're sharing before clicking the "share" button. If your partner knew about it, do you think they'd rather you kept quiet? Finding a middle ground on which you can both feel comfortable is essential if you want to reach a compromise. When in doubt, ask your partner, especially if you already know that privacy is a major issue for them. Set limits on how much personal information may be shared on social media before a fight occurs.

Ask Yourself Why You Want To Share

It's not uncommon for Facebook profiles to portray a seemingly perfect couple or family, but these facades may be deceiving. What are you writing a gushing post about your significant other for? The two of you, or the world at large?

If you are posting to get your partner's attention or affection, you should have a conversation with them instead of resorting to the web.

Don't Type What You Don't Want Your Spouse To See

Can social media really destroy a friendship or romance? When used in an inappropriate manner, yes. Think about the individuals you're following on social media, especially any exes or ex-lovers you may still feel some nostalgic pull toward.

You shouldn't keep up a running direct message with someone you wouldn't flirt with in person. Would you really tell your partner the things you write about them? Do not say anything on social media if the answer is no.

As harmless as online flirting may seem, it often leads to real-world feelings and, in some cases, actual physical intimacy. To avoid this, be selective when selecting your friends and remember to always keep your talks tasteful.

Tip: Always consider how you would feel if your partner were posting the same content as you.

Come To An Agreement About Sharing Passwords Or Accounts

No one likes to feel like a nosy neighbor, yet social media accounts may be hard to resist. One study found that trust was directly associated to account sharing (but relationship satisfaction was not).

While it's crucial to have faith in your partner's social media habits, it's also essential to have a conversation about how you handle passing on secrets. Many couples choose to have open-door policies on social media to convey trust to one another.

You and your spouse may not be good candidates for the shared-password method. However, you may discover that giving your partner access makes you feel better about what you say and who you say it to, or it may make you more careful, which is not a terrible thing if it means stopping you from talking to people who can harm your relationship. If you're worried about your spouse cheating, it's crucial that you talk to them about it instead of violating their privacy.

Tip: Ask what your significant other thinks about sharing passwords. Is this important?

Exercise Accountability

Most people don't start out wanting to stray in their relationships. Most committed couples are just that—committed, at least at the onset when everything is new and exciting. When we start breaking down barriers in our online and social media conversations, that's when things may become complicated. You may find this especially troublesome if you and your partner are currently experiencing difficulties. Do not discuss your relationship issues with strangers online; instead, talk to your partner, a trusted confidant, or a competent therapist.

It's a good idea to avoid having private conversations with someone who can tempt you to have an affair, whether it be emotional or physical. This is more of a rule of thumb than a hard and strict regulation. People often develop close relationships with those they have romantic feelings for. The most crucial factor is that your significant other is aware of your friendship and that you explicitly know they don't have any suspicions about it. Do not assume anything; rather, inquire.

Setting Social Media Boundaries In Relationships

Rather than asking for more than either of you can provide, you've come to an understanding of how much each of you can do for the other. You may, for instance, try not using your phone at all on dates to see how it goes. When it's feasible, schedule daily phone-free time to focus only on your significant other. You can, for instance, give each other some time during dinner or an hour before bed. But this is a sweet activity that will help you stay in love with each other.

Try something new as a team, like a sport or board game you both can enjoy. Get involved in a new activity, like a cooking course or couple's yoga. Some couples do well with shared screen time. Playing the same game repeatedly may become boring, even for the most dedicated gamers.

Find a degree of privacy that suits both of you: Determine what is off-limits and what you're comfortable discussing.

Whatever you and your partner do, do it to strengthen your relationship rather than just figure out a way to keep your social media use out of sight and hidden. You should revisit the conversation if you discover that the understanding isn't working. Even if your trust in each other is unwavering, it's still a good idea to have a conversation about where the two of you stand when it comes to using social media.

Tip: Think about establishing time restrictions or boundaries for your usage of social media and electronics, especially while spending time with your significant other.

These are by no means exhaustive suggestions for social media etiquette; yet they may be useful as jumping-off points for meaningful discussions. The simple act of discussing these concepts with a significant other may often make all the difference.

Having open and frank discussions about these issues may also help reduce misunderstandings and tensions.

Give Your Partner The Benefit Of The Doubt

Remember all the reasons you fell in love with this human, and why they matter so much to you. Even if you come across suspicious activity by accident, keep in mind that tone and intent are far more difficult to assess online. As a species, we tend to make snap judgments based on little evidence. Clarifying your partner's intentions before acting on any assumptions you may have is important. For instance: *"Hey, I saw you're now Facebook friends with the girl you told me you hooked up with before we met. How did that come about?"*

Pay attention to what they say and look for cues that suggest guilt or innocence. Maybe they aren't being entirely truthful. If you're having trouble making up your mind, take your time before taking any action, but don't torment yourself into believing that everyone you meet is out to get you.

Chapter 12
Establish Mutual Communication

One of the toughest things you will find as a single woman in a vast world is that not everyone will emote or experience emotions the same way you do. Many people will be wonderful in who they are, but there may be those ever-so-slight indications that they aren't right for you. And this is one of the biggest truths of life— so many people we get involved with are not bad in that sense of the term, *they're simply bad for us.* Emotional bonding is crucial in any relationship, and when it comes to matters of the heart, it is perhaps the sole indicator that you are building something that will last.

Defining Emotional Connection

Everyone has their own unique idea of what constitutes an emotional connection, yet there is a universally applicable definition. A bond between two individuals may be said to exist when they have a strong attachment, which is a collection of shared, personal experiences. When we talk about something being "emotional," we mean the act of experiencing something that makes us feel deeply.

A human being can experience thousands of different feelings, some of which include wrath, sadness, joy, and love. A connection is an association between two entities.

When you combine the words "emotion" and "connection," you get the feeling that you're tied to that person because you share the same series of emotions and in the same frequencies as them. Let's face it, it's hard to be in a relationship where you find you are much more in love with your partner than they can be with you. And it's not their fault, they are just wired differently. For this reason, you need to ensure you are with someone who can match the same rhythm of your heart to their own.

Relationships Without An Emotional Connection

A relationship becomes a battlefield when the emotional connection is out of whack. You are always on opposite ends of the spectrum, and a time will come when you begin resenting your partner for their inability to love as you do.

Perhaps you have found someone to share your life with whom you feel passionately or adore deeply. On the other hand, they come out as cold and aloof, reluctant to open up about their innermost thoughts and feelings.

This connection might be platonic, as in a friendship, or it could be more committed, as in a cohabitation or sexual arrangement. In the absence of a solid emotional connection, the relationship is doomed to disappoint at least one of the participants.

Signs of Emotional Connection

Emotional connection is not about having superficial conversations or banking on surface-level similarities to keep a relationship going. It is about genuinely feeling a deep sense of attachment, respect, and care for the other person. As you can imagine, an intense emotional connection lays the foundation for long-term and real intimacy.

If you want to build a sustainable and happy relationship, being emotionally connected is key. And there are some telltale signs pointing to a healthy partnership that abounds in this form of attachment:

- You feel comfortable showing how big your love for them is because you know they won't be overwhelmed or think you are too much.

- You share funny stories of what happened at work and bad days when everything went wrong.

- You are both willing to give each other peeks into childhood dreams and adult aspirations.

- The conversation flows easily between both of you.

Even in silence, a couple creating a strong emotional bond will feel at ease. You can share anything with your partner without fear that they will flee, and they feel the same. This can be a deep conversation to just lying side-by-side, each of you doing your own thing in companionable silence.

- You may feel "butterflies" in her stomach each time they call. They may finish your sentence or start speaking the same thought simultaneously.

Although one may lead to the next, physical attraction is a superficial emotion that begins the journey toward an emotional connection and love. It is a part of emotional connection, but not essential to it. Of course, when your physical attachment comes with both of you feeling truly fulfilled and bonded with each other, intimacy can be the icing on the cake to a lasting association.

How To Establish An Mutual Connection

Determining how connected you are to each other in the early stages of a new relationship is challenging. Perhaps you're wondering whether or not your partner feels the same level of commitment to the relationship as you do. Maybe you've hit it off physically, but you're still wondering whether there's anything more going on.

Instead of worrying about whether or whether your relationship with your partner looks good to the world, focus on how strong it is and how well it fits into your life. Think about the various ways in which couples might connect: physically, mentally, emotionally, spiritually, and socially.

Is there a connection between you and your partner in many different aspects of your lives? In what ways does it manifest itself in each area? Where exactly is it lacking? Examine your relationship through the lens of these five touchstones to find out where you stand:

You can connect on an emotional level.

For an emotional connection to flourish, both parties must be open and honest about their sentiments, even the more sensitive ones like sadness, fear, humiliation, or isolation. Your relationship may need more time to mature if you aren't emotionally open with one other, or you may be dating someone who isn't emotionally expressive.

Keep in mind that the first few months of a relationship might seem quite euphoric, with both partners experiencing intense feelings for one another. This emotion is most likely caused by the feel-good chemicals released in your brain while you're falling in love. It's the same as getting a new dress or a promotion. But the relationship will also grow old over time, like the dress and the job post.

When it does, you need to be sure your connection goes beyond the level of superficiality. Developing a solid emotional bond requires commitment and patience, so nourish your relationship with both.

This must be a two-way street. You may not have the connection necessary for a healthy relationship if you have tremendous feelings for them but get the sense that they don't feel the same way.

The best way to figure out whether you have a genuine emotional connection with someone is to have open, honest talks about how you feel about the relationship and each other.

You build social connections similarly.

How would you describe your social relationship with each other? How do you and your partner relate to the world, both individually and collectively? A strong social bond may be established when two people have the same interests in activities, hobbies, and even ways of life.

Do you spend time doing these things together, and do you find that you enjoy each other's company? Do you get to know your partner's friends and family members?

Relationship dynamics are also key determinants of social connection. It may be a good complement and balance for the relationship if one of you is more introverted and the other is more extroverted, but it can also cause a rift if the two of you have very different personalities. Consider your connections to one another and the world at large. You're in luck if you think you and the other person can get along well as friends.

You think and process things similarly.

Do you share my outlook on things? Your dates with someone who doesn't think in analytical, intellectual ways may leave you feeling bored if you're into stimulating conversations. While physical closeness blossoms in the early stages of a relationship, the beauty of an established emotional connection makes the passing of the years no less enjoyable.

If you and your spouse can't converse freely about the things that really interest you, then you won't be able to build a strong connection with one another. If you're looking to make some new connections, finding someone with similar intellectual interests as you might be helpful.

Your chemistry is undeniable.

A lot of your initial time with a potential partner will be hinged on how you connect physically. But I'd take a pause here and say even if it doesn't feel electric, consider if it makes you feel warm and wholesome.

If your relationship is lacking in other areas, you may worry that physicality is all there is to it. Although it's nice when two people click on a physical level, that alone may not be enough to make a relationship seem genuine or safe. Take time to assess where you stand on other areas, but also know that clicking on a physical level can contribute to the closeness you share-- especially if it means you get to spend more time just talking about life or being close with each other.

You feel like you're MEANT to be together.

Have you met a kindred spirit? Depending on your spiritual beliefs or faith, this could be an important piece of a relationship.

You may have found each other for a reason if you have a strong emotional connection. A common sentiment is to believe that fate or divine intervention brought two people together. This connection has several layers. There are many ways to feel close to someone, and the factors that matter the most to you in a relationship may vary depending on your individuality and your expectations.

The stronger the quality and quantity of your connections, the greater your chances of having a successful long-term relationship.

If you and your partner aren't emotionally connected, being together might make you feel unhappy. And your discomfort would be valid. Something is missing in this scenario: the firm link that binds two people together and grows into a love that endures through the years.

Chapter 13
Set Healthy Limits

Given the current state of the world, you may be spending more time than ever with your partner. If you find that you are together a lot, it may not always be easy to set the necessary limits to spending time with each other. Perhaps you have already set healthy boundaries for your relationship, but they have been hard to maintain. Setting thresholds (or reevaluating them) in your relationship will ultimately help reduce stress and ensure that you have a healthy dynamic with your partner.

You may, and probably do, love your partner dearly. Even so, spending every minute of every day in the presence of another human can get challenging, especially if you begin to feel you have no time to yourself. Rather than bottling up this issue and then getting angry (which ultimately leads to ugly fights), consider setting down healthy boundaries at the onset.

Six Tips For Setting Healthy Boundaries

Before establishing limits, think about the reasons why they matter to you. Setting clear limits between you and your partner is essential for a happy relationship. They aid in reducing arguments by setting a standard for how you should behave towards one another. Boundaries, when established via open dialogue, have the potential to strengthen your relationship with your partner.

People with a poor sense of boundaries either take too much responsibility for the actions and emotions of others or expect others to do everything for them. Suppose there is a relationship between two people where one constantly blames their partner and expects them to take care of everything. At the same time, the other keeps trying extra hard to satisfy their every whim. In that case, you know you are headed to a disaster city.

Interestingly, the *"I'll get you to do everything for me and still blame you"* type people and the *"I'll do anything you ask me to"* type people often end up together and destroy each other. I'd hope that given everything you have learned; you will choose to take a step back from this trap. The last thing you want right now is a partner who doesn't let you have your own life and who whines every time you make plans with friends and family.

Be Honest About What You Need

Transparent communication is a crucial component of every loving relationship. Being open and honest with your partner about what you're comfortable with and how you can help them understand what you're looking for in a companion. You may try writing down your expectations so that there's no room for error, or you could introduce them by way of a natural conversation and let them know what stage of life you are at.

Listen to What Your Partner Needs

You want your partner to respect your limits, therefore it's only fair that you do the same for them. It's crucial to acknowledge the other person's space and discuss any boundaries they want to put in the relationship. Remember that in a relationship, you may say anything, but the way you say it is what really counts. So yes, while you must let your voice and requirements be heard, neither of you can nor should be blunt about it. Let the conversation flow until a time comes when you move to discussing where you want to take the relationship. Give them your full, honest take, and invite the same from them.

Designate When You Need Space

The current climate makes this approach particularly relevant, with many people on lockdown or working from home. Be sure to communicate with each other about when you need time apart if you're currently spending a lot of time together. Setting aside time for yourself is just as important as spending quality time with the ones you love, so always leave room to breathe for your inner peace.

Establish How Comfortable You Are In the Scope of COVID-19

Your social expectations and the limits within which you interact with friends and family may have shifted throughout this time. If you haven't already, you and your significant other should talk about how comfortable you are with being around other people in terms of sharing space and any other relevant context.

The key lies in sharing your space comfortably, so you don't end up fighting about how suffocated you feel. Take time to go on walks while maintaining safety protocols, and do activities that you love by yourself while sharing some hobbies with your partner.

Communicate With Respect

Respect on both sides is essential to maintaining a good connection. Empathy, understanding, and regard for each other's expectations are the best tools for conveying your limits to your partner. Maintaining a healthy and strong relationship requires both parties to treat one another with compassion in every interaction.

Boundaries To Protect

Dating after divorce can be a lot of fun. The prospects! The possibilities! An entire world of chances is now yours for the taking— but, it may be stressful to try to balance your own post-divorce needs and goals with those of a potential new partner. Potential for muddled thinking to set in. It's possible you'll experience feelings of isolation and vulnerability. If you don't want to feel taken advantage of or regret not setting firm boundaries from the start, it's crucial to do so. Here are six.

Your Body

Act as though your body were your most prized treasure. That means protecting it as if your life depended on it, since one mistake might cost you your life or at least the quality of it. Don't take the importance of protection lightly. If you engage in sexual activity, you should be tested regularly for sexually transmitted infections. Never force yourself into a sexual situation you aren't ready for, and don't let anybody else do the same. If you don't trust yourself and think you'll act impulsively, avoid situations where that may happen. Just admitting that you're not prepared is perfectly OK. If you aren't ready, say no. And if they react childishly, give them the boot. They're not worth your while.

Your Time

Time, like your body, is a finite resource. Don't ever allow somebody the opportunity to squander your time. Included in it is the time spent dwelling on someone who doesn't merit your thoughts. If the person you're seeing isn't giving you the attention you need, is chronically late, repeatedly bails on plans, or otherwise tries to keep you on the hook by checking in and making bogus promises, it's time to cut ties and move on. You shouldn't stay in a relationship that leaves you unhappy.

Reevaluate your position and consider other options. Time is a valuable resource, and the more you squander, the less you have to spend on yourself or other important. Remember that this time around, you are dating someone because you want to—not out of any obligations. So, if it's not worth your time, he's not worthy of you.

Your Money

It's a cliche to say, but love costs just as much as any other commodity. It's not cheap to maintain meaningful personal relationships. Everything has a monetary value, from the date itself to travel time to the opportunity cost of spending your resources elsewhere. Speak out if you think the power dynamic between you and your partner in the economy is unfair.

Money is one of the most prevalent sources of tension in relationships, particularly those rekindled after separation or divorce. Your partner's or potential partner's view of the financial picture may differ from your own. The only way to avoid misunderstandings is to talk about money and expectations as soon as possible.

Your Sanity

Every kind of person may be manipulated or emotionally abused. Unfortunately, seasoned manipulators often come off as pleasant, complimentary, supportive, and lovely at first acquaintance. However, a manipulator will not be able to keep up appearances forever, so a time will come when things won't seem so "sunny". Hear what your intuition tells you.

If you're feeling uneasy about a guy because his words and deeds don't line up and think he's gaslighting you whenever you point out something that's amiss, reconsider being with them. Examine why you feel the way you do considering his subtle (or not-so-subtle) jabs at your appearance, profession, body, or anything else of value to you. You're probably not the one who thinks this world is upside down. He is.

Your Heart

There's a verse in the Bible that tells us, "*above all else, guard your heart, for everything you do flows from it.*" (Proverbs 4:23, NIV) Falling in love is "*ethereal*"; that is when you fall in love with someone who loves and treats you well. When you fall in love with someone who treats you poorly, doesn't show you respect, or fails to care for you in the ways you need and deserve, the heartache you will experience can negatively affect how you see the world and, in turn, permeate every aspect of your life. The love you have to give is a gift. Bestow it wisely.

Your Dignity

When you let the person you're seeing cross any of the essential boundaries, they're chipping away at what should be your most solid defense: your individuality. You deserve a partner worthy of you since you are unique and special. Don't ever allow somebody to change you; instead, know your worth and stick to it.

Protecting Yourself Financially

It can be hard to control your urges when you are in a new relationship with someone, and they are everything you'd ever hoped for. They treat you well, give you the kind of love and attention that was missing from your life, and don't miss any opportunity to make you feel special. Then, one day, they call you up and say they need a substantial amount of money. But you think they'd never ask unless it was really serious and trust they will return it to you once they have access to the cash again.

They say a payment is being withheld or their bank has messed up with something, and you, in the throes of passionate love, don't stop to consider how ridiculous the excuses may sound. So you give them the money. It's fine for about ten days, and then they ask again. Except this time, it's for a larger sum. This goes on until one day, you find you need to take a loan if you are to help him any further. *Don't be this person.*

Look out for these financial nuances at the onset of your relationship. If your partner fits the description for any or multiple of these, you should reconsider your choices.

Refusal to split money

If your partner shows little to zero inclination to share expenses after even five dates, you can take it as a sign of what is to come. Either they are not serious about being seen with you, or they're expecting you to take care of their financial needs for the rest of their lives. The lack of willingness to split money is reflective of their lack of respect for your commitment and time. Still, it could also point to something more serious like their inability to handle or manage their own finances. The person can also be a freeloader who isn't entirely invested in the relationship. In all these cases, it's a good idea to run before it becomes too late and too heavy on your wallet.

Lying about money

As with other forms of infidelity, financial adultery caused by lying may end a relationship completely. Your date's dishonesty with money matters may extend to other areas of your life as well if they have lied to you about other topics. Lies may be on a sliding scale, from something as simple as keeping some money under your mattress to something as elaborate as hiding debt, exaggerating earnings, or keeping certain transactions or accounts private.

It may have dire repercussions, such as disrupting the budget or preventing retirement savings from being accumulated. When one spouse lies about an impulsive action, it's usually because they feel bad about it, want to rebel against their partner's dominating behavior, or are afraid of their partner's response. Whatever the case is, it will hurt your relationship if your partner continuously lies about their earnings and spending.

Doesn't talk about money

If you've been dating for a while and are ready to take things to the next level, but your partner is still unwilling to talk about money, that's a huge red flag. It's normal to feel uncomfortable bringing about money early in a relationship. It would be even more so if your date showed an unusually strong interest in your finances. Even after a few years of relationship, showing signs of hesitation, impatience, or rage while discussing finances is cause for concern.

The inability to handle money and admitting it to the partner might be the root cause of the reluctance to address it, as could a desire to maintain financial control in the union. The unwillingness to communicate might stem from insecurity or rebellion if a man's income is lower than a woman's. However, if you see this behavior in its early stages, you would be unwise not to take corrective measures.

Borrows excessively from you

Do you dread the end of the month because your significant other always seems to want a helping hand to get through it? Be wary if (s)he is always cash-strapped and asking for bridging loans from you or his parents. Spending more money than you get in on a regular basis is not acceptable, while a temporary cash flow problem is okay.

Your financial situation will spiral out of control if you continue to mismanage your money and not set aside any savings. If your spouse is constantly asking you or your family for financial assistance, it's time for them to start making changes, including finding better employment.

Small, repeated borrowings of money without repayment may be a sign of financial carelessness and dependency on others, both of which can lead to bigger problems and substantial debt. Overstepping one's financial limits in a relationship is problematic and should be avoided.

At the end of the day, your finances should be in a place that allows both of you to live comfortably without feeling completely exhausted by each other's spending habits. With all these boundaries in place, you will be well on your way to a healthy, wholesome relationship.

Chapter 14

Keep Your Dignity Intact

Many years back, when I was in a new relationship, I remember a day when I came home from work. It was late in the evening, and I wanted to order takeout because I was really tired. Now, at the time, the man I was dating was— to all appearances— a good guy. So, I was certain we could just kick back with pizza and a couple of beers and talk about how our day had gone.

He tells me to make him dinner as soon as I step out of the shower. I told him I was tired and just wanted to rest. His response? *"You can rest after dinner too, right? I mean, like cooking should just come naturally to you."* I was flabbergasted back then, and I did what he asked, but looking back, I know he impinged on my dignity. I shouldn't have let him. But it was an experience well learned.

Maintaining a sense of dignity while dealing with the complexity of relations is the toughest challenge in almost everyone's lives. The health of relationships, be it personal or professional, depends on mutual love and respect. So to have worthy relationships, you all need to treat your partner with respect, and at the same time, you also need to keep your dignity intact.

No one wants to be treated badly. It is the birthright of everyone to feel worthy, deserving, and live with dignity. If your partner can't give you the respect you deserve, the relationship won't hold itself together simply because sooner or later you'll tire of it.

Maintain Mutual Respect

Strong relationships are built on trust, open communication, and a willingness to put in the effort to get to know one another. For every relationship to thrive, its members must be able to read and accommodate the needs and preferences of one another.

Together, you may learn to understand and respect one another so that you can both feel good about yourself and treat your spouse with the respect you deserve. Living with respect makes both partners feel valued. That's why mutual respect is so crucial to the health of any relationship.

Do Not Compromise On Dignity

In a relationship, each partner needs to draw boundaries as to how much they are willing to give. Everyone requires little distance and a sense of self-respect for their individual growth.

You cannot thrive in a situation where you are forced to do things against your true nature.

Dignity is about being worthy of honor and respect for yourself. To have dignity is to have high self-esteem and, at the same time, honor the other person also. It is self-expression to carry oneself respectfully and is a core of everyone's aspirations.

Hence, do not compromise your dignity to keep the relationship going. If you bend over backwards to please your partner, you will keep your dignity at stake and make yourself vulnerable to losing your individuality. Maybe it won't seem bad on day one or even ten, but over time, you will erode all sense of self.

Live With Dignity

A dignified life is one in which one treats oneself and others with respect. No matter what challenges you confront, remember to be level-headed and take care of business without sacrificing your integrity.

Keeping your pride and self-respect intact will serve as a source of inspiration no matter how challenging the situation becomes. The people in your life may come and go at various points, and your financial situation may be excellent or bad, but your dignity is the one constant that may provide you lasting happiness.

Someone who lacks pride loses all respect from others around them. A lack of dignity makes one susceptible to manipulation and abuse. Therefore, it is essential to always retain a certain level of self-respect; otherwise, others will be willing to take advantage of you.

Happiness may be attained through living a life of respect for oneself. It has nothing to do with your social standing or financial stability. Believing in yourself is all that's required; knowing your value and accepting yourself as you are will get you through life's challenges, no matter how difficult they are.

Hence, while dealing with the complexity of partnerships, always ensure sure you do not trade your dignity in exchange for getting your partner's attention and love. Your dignity is the foundation of being an unique person in this world, and it was with you even before your partner came into your existence.

Keep your dignity intact even if you're forced to make a morally ambiguous decision. You are an independent individual first and a partner later, not the otherwise. Maintaining your individuality in a relationship is important for both partners to feel appreciated and for the partnership as a whole to thrive.

Love Has A Limit, And Its Name Is Dignity

The respect we each have for ourselves is priceless, and it will never do to accept a love that isn't satisfying hurts and leaves us vulnerable. Therefore, love must always factor in dignity.

Love is fleeting but forgetting lasts a lifetime. So then, in between, there is always that "firefly's light" that naturally flares up in the nights to show us where the limit is, to remind us that it is better to spend a long time forgetting than in a long torment where we end up selling our dignity. In other words, don't rush into a new relationship out of fear and compromise your self-respect in the process. Wait for something good to come along.

After all, love should not be something we are forced to beg for or just snatch as hurriedly as possible. We must never put our pride before of our love, but we also sell our dignity by way of love.

Whether we want to admit it or not, dignity is a frail, delicate string that may snap after being strained just once too often, and this can have a negative impact on our interpersonal relationships. Sometimes we cross that line unintentionally. Our weak moral reasoning causes us to get swept away by extremes. We consider any sacrifice we make for love to be inconsequential. Because love and dignity are two currents in a fierce ocean, even the most experienced sailor can lose his way. Remember that time seasons you and teaches you to choose what is right. Let it be your friend.

The Pride And Dignity Of Self-Love

It is often said that the ego feeds our pride and the spirit our dignity. Whatever the case may be, these two psychological dimensions are two daily inhabitants of the complex islands of our emotional relationships, and sometimes they end up confusing us.

Pride, for example, is an enemy that we know all too well and it tends to be associated with self-love. Nevertheless, it goes a step beyond this because pride is an architect specializing in building walls and weaving entanglements of barbed wire in our relationships, flourishing every detail with arrogance, and cleaving victimization to every word. However, underneath all of these destructive actions, low self-esteem is hidden. We only fall back on pride when we are too afraid of our insecurities.

As for dignity, it is the exact opposite. It acts by listening to the voice of our inner selves at all times. We learn to foster self-respect without forgetting about respect for others. Here, the concept of self-love acquires its maximum meaning because we feed on it to protect ourselves without harming others. Essentially, we validate our self-esteem without causing collateral damage.

Dignity Has A Very High Price

A defeat at the right time is worth more than a victory if we are able to walk away from it with our pride intact and our honor intact.

Resignation and martyrdom have no place in a healthy and worthwhile love relationship. When we join them in the shadows, there won't be much light to warm our hearts or hope to sustain us. To escape these pervasive emotional currents, it's important to take stock of your own feelings about love and why you want to be in a committed partnership with another person.

Sacrifices in emotional relationships have limits that should be clearly delineated. We are not obligated to solve all of our partner's problems, to give them a lungful of air every time they take a breath, or to dim our own light so that theirs may shine brighter. Remember that the true boundary is inside your own individuality.

Love is felt, touched, and created every day. If we do not perceive any of these things, it will not serve any purpose to ask for it, and even less so to sit there waiting for a miracle that makes no sense.

Love must never be blind. No matter how much this idea is defended in society, it is necessary to remember that it is always better to offer oneself to someone with eyes wide open, a heart lit up, and very strong dignity. You *must* know what you're getting into.

Dignity is and always will be the recognition that we are worthy of better things. It will always be better to have dignified solitude than a life with incomplete relationships. Do not permit it. Do not lose your dignity over anybody.

How To Gain More Power

There are power dynamics at play in every type of relationship. So it should come as no surprise that there will be a power dynamic in your romantic relationship. There is an equal amount of power and respect in some partnerships, and in others, one partner holds most of the power.

The power can shift at different points in your relationship to make things even more complicated. Maybe you two never thought of power and respect in the beginning because it felt equally distributed. But then, as time went on, you noticed things shifting, and you felt like your boyfriend or girlfriend somehow had more power. Wait a second, weren't you the Beyonce of this couple? How did a situation come where the power just shifted?

It's normal for the power dynamic to shift in a relationship. Many things could have made the partnership structure change. But once it has swayed into a new direction (the one you may not be fond of), how do you get on equal footing? If your man has gotten a little too "Kanye West" on you, how do you gain more power and respect in the relationship? How do you turn this ship around and sail towards a more peaceful and happy sea where the tides are even?

Below are some ways to gain more power and respect in your romantic relationship.

Speak up

One way to become more powerful is to use your voice. Be clear about your wants and needs. If you don't speak up for yourself, who else will? Remember, your partner can't read your mind. Therefore, you need to use your words and tell them what you want and need in your partnership.

Be more independent

You still need your partner even if you're strong and independent. It only demonstrates that you are a capable person who can make things happen on your own. Having the ability to take care of yourself while still being in a committed relationship is essential. You and your partner will both be impressed by your level of autonomy.

Have boundaries

Everyone is at ease inside their own rules and boundaries. You and your partner need to set and adhere to clear limits in your relationship. It's important to be able to draw a firm line when something is beyond your own threshold of acceptability.

The golden rule

Stick to the golden rule. One simple method of gaining respect is to treat your spouse the way you would want to be treated. Respect and consideration are earned by showing them to those who deserve them, such as your significant other.

Follow through on your word

You might quickly lose someone's respect if you tell them one thing but do another. For better or worse, deeds speak louder than words, particularly in interpersonal relationships. If you tell your partner there will be consequences for something and then don't deliver, they won't take you seriously. And if you make even a little promise to your partner, do your best to honor your word. Always be honest and forthright in your communication.

Do not settle

There's nothing more confident and attractive than somebody who knows what they deserve. If you're in a relationship where your partner knows they can get away with anything, your power and respect have already gone out the window. Stand up for yourself, and don't be afraid to walk away from a relationship that doesn't benefit you.

Respect yourself

Who else will respect you if you don't respect yourself? It begins with yourself. You have to show how you want to be treated. A reflection of this will be in your treatment of yourself. To what extent do you discuss yourself in conversation? A key question is whether you believe in your own power. How do you feel about yourself? Give some thought to your honest opinion of yourself. Keep in mind that assurance is contagious.

Chapter 15
Build A Solid Foundation

A relationship with a significant other is like a house built on sand: without a firm foundation, it will eventually collapse. This may not be very groundbreaking for some people, but for others it represents a crucial step in comprehending the nature of a base.

A fulfilling relationship and outcome may be considered as having a solid foundation. And much like a house with shaky or severely cracked flooring, roofing, or walls, it can't stand up straight or provide shelter in the first place if the foundation isn't there.

Establishing a foundation of mutual appreciation, trust, respect, compassion, shared goals, open communication, and forgiveness in every relationship is crucial. This takes time to cultivate, particularly given the fluidity with which individuals and groups define connections during their travels.

The foundation, however, must be what keeps the couple together through the highs and lows. Having a mutual interest in self-improvement and spiritual development is crucial, as is the recognition that you're both on a journey to discover your purpose in this world.

How To Start Building Or Reinforcing That Foundation

Grow Together in Self-Development

Suppose you are both passionate about educating yourself, especially in self-development and spiritual growth. In that case, that is the foundation you can always come back to. It gives you the best chance for the union to have longevity. In addition, numerous studies have found that the relationships and marriages that last the longest are those where the partners have similar core values and beliefs.

Create a Never-ending Honeymoon Phase

Even when the so-called honeymoon period appears to be over, there's no reason it can't continue. But the only way it's going to do this is if:

- You have similarly wholesome beliefs about relationships.

- You understand why you are going into the relationship.

- Your partner shares your core values

By their very nature, whether it's material possessions, sex, or something else, everything has a habit of changing and fading in life. So you want to look at ways of coming back to the foundation because that's the thing that is unchangeable and will keep you together.

Perceive Relationships the Right Way

The divorce rate throughout the world is staggering, that much is evident. However, I believe this is due to the widespread dissemination of a false idea or fantasy that romantic partnerships are analogous to the Cinderella narrative. People often look to their partners to fulfill emotional needs that they feel they don't have in their own lives.

Realize that your partner is not the one who will make you happy; happiness is something you create for yourself. This is the ideal technique for establishing and maintaining a satisfying romantic connection. You're on a voyage, and it's wonderful to have a soulmate to go with.

Love Unconditionally

Having no expectations, not passing judgment, and gaining insight into the unconditional nature of love are the cornerstones of a strong relationship. That is, loving someone but yet allowing them to live their own lives.

We try to control our partner much too frequently. Continuously loving and letting go is at the heart of unconditional love. To accept and love someone also means accepting and loving the things about them that we don't like.

Look Within

When you're in a healthy relationship, your partner will reflect to you on the areas of yourself that need healing. However, if you refuse to examine such matters, you are more likely to avoid them. You could want to avoid these things because you don't enjoy looking at the parts of yourself that need healing. It's more probable that you'll point the blame upon your spouse and tell them, "*Figure it out; it's your thing.*"

The trick is to examine your own reflection to determine what needs your attention, since this is probably something you need to own up to. When seen in this light, the connection between the two becomes clear as one of development and evolution, one that ultimately serves to strengthen and unite the two.

Choose Love, Not Fear

When it comes down to it, most people are terrified of love, even though it is the most beautiful thing there is. The only things that are present in the world are love and fear. It is essential that you do not place the blame for your fears on your partner. As I've said in the past, you must first learn to love yourself and figure out how to express that love in a genuinely.

Of course, this might be challenging since any fears you may have are likely more deeply rooted. Again, giving things time is crucial to finding a healthy relationship. First, heal yourself, then look for external gratification. The foundation of our relationships with both ourselves and others may be strengthened by developing an understanding of and coming to terms with the emotions involved.

Chapter 16

Co-Parenting Boundaries

When you co-parent, your child has one biological parent and one step-parent. It's a family unit becoming more and more common, and if you're about to become a blended family, you're not alone!

Blended families can be brilliant for little ones, and some step-parents can become as important as biological parents. But that doesn't mean it will be easy for you, your new partner, or your children. One of the biggest challenges in blended families is setting co-parenting boundaries with your new partner without hurting your children.

What Is Co-Parenting?

Let's define co-parenting before diving into the advice.

Co-parenting is when one or both of a child's biological parents works with the other to raise the child. You're both responsible for taking care of your kids and have input into important decisions about their upbringing. When you're co-parenting, you and your partner take on equal responsibilities for your child.

This kind of co-parenting arrangement is often straightforward in families with two biological parents who are still together. It's a rather simple method, albeit hiccups are possible. When parents divorce, though, the system may become more complex.

Co-parenting is a challenge that many divorced or single parents experience while raising their children. Giving up some control over your children to someone who isn't your biological parent may be difficult, and young children may struggle to respect their authority. This is why it's crucial to establish ground rules and ensure that everyone is satisfied with the new co-parenting arrangement.

The Three Relationships

When you find a new partner as a divorced or single parent, there are three relationships you need to take care of.

The first relationship is with the other biological parent. Although they may not be your partner anymore, you still have a relationship with them and a responsibility to consider them in parenting decisions. Keeping them in the loop is essential to a smooth transition into co-parenting in new relationships.

The second relationship is with your new partner. They may struggle with having a new child in their lives, and you need to be careful to keep them happy with the dynamic, too. You also need to ensure there is a comfortable dynamic between your ex and your partner— and that the ex doesn't make snide comments or snub them when they come to spend time with your kids.

The relationship you have with your child is the most significant and final one. For the sake of your child's happiness, you, your ex, and your new spouse should all work together for the best of everyone involved. We'll talk more about how to keep your child at the forefront of your mind while you negotiate the complexities of co-parenting in a little while.

Keep in mind that it's not enough to ensure the contentment of these three individuals; you need to do the same for yourself. You are equally important, so be sure to put yourself in a comfortable place.

All parties involved in such relationships should feel like they have a voice in the co-parenting decisions being made. Think about how your boundary setting will influence each person involved. Let's delve into the ways in which you and your new partner may establish healthy boundaries.

Talk to Your Ex

Before establishing boundaries with your new relationship, it's a good idea to have a conversation with the other biological parent (for simplicity's sake, we'll refer to this person as your exes, even if they may not be). Every time you bring a new person into your parenting dynamic, it's important to talk about how much of a say they should have in shaping your child's upbringing. Discuss with your ex how involved they would like this new partner to be and how they feel about interacting with your new partner.

If your ex is unhappy about you dating again, it's best to keep them at arm's length. Don't bring a new date to drop-offs and pick-ups, to parent-specific events (like school plays), and don't mention them often until the relationship is serious. Of course, after things get serious, you have every right to bring your partner along. If the ex still causes issues then, a conversation about boundaries with them is warranted because they have no right to impinge on your happiness.

If your ex-spouse is okay with the friendship you've maintained, you'll have more leeway to talk freely about co-parenting. Communicate openly with them about your new partner's involvement in your child's life, seek their advice, and tell them about any limits you plan to put in place. Even if you and your ex are likely well-versed in co-parenting at this point, it never hurts to hear some fresh perspective.

Talk to Your Children

Your child is the most important person (or people) to consider here. Before introducing a new partner into their life, make sure you talk to them, and never force a partner onto your little ones. That doesn't mean you can't have a relationship if your child isn't happy with it, but don't force them to spend time with the new partner or be happy with them – it'll be much easier if they can do that in their own time.

Make changes slowly, and always keep your little ones involved. Start with a small meeting in a park or somewhere your child is happy and familiar with. Get them used to your new partner before inviting them into your home, and ensure your children know that they are still your priority.

You can discuss boundaries with your child, too, as long as they're old enough. Ask them what kind of relationship they hope to have with your new partner once it's serious and what things your new partner could do without overstepping your child's boundaries. Be sensitive to these and make your partner aware of your child's feelings.

Know Your Boundaries

When co-parenting, it's natural to put other people's needs before your own. But remember that boundary-setting is ultimately about you. Spend some time thinking about how involved in your child's life you want your new partner to be. Here are some questions to ask yourself that should help you establish your limits:

- Would it be okay to leave your children alone with your new partner?

- Are you okay with your partner disciplining your children?

- Do you want your new partner at school meetings involving your children?

- Will you take advice on parenting from your new partner?

Knowing what you expect from your new partner is essential. Consider if it would be safe to let them move in with you and your child if you are unhappy with the strong parental role they are taking. Can you leave them alone if you don't approve of how they are disciplining your child?

If you've already answered these questions for yourself, then it's time to have a conversation with your co-parenting partner about establishing boundaries.

Be Honest With Your New Partner

You should be open and honest with your new partner about your child right away. Tell your partner that your child is your top priority and that they will always come before them in any situation. If your partner objects to this, you may need to reevaluate whether or not this is the correct relationship for you. However, you should assure them that they are important as well, and that you will make sure to set aside plenty of quality time for the relationship.

You should initiate the meeting between your child and your new partner after you feel comfortable in your relationship. This will Now is a great time to test your partner's tolerance for time-sharing and family activities. It's fantastic if they're up for it!

Plan out the logistics of the meeting and remind your new partner not to be too forward with your child. In order to build lasting bonds, you must be patient. Never force a new partner on your children; if it's serious, it's worth waiting for your kid to warm up to the idea on his or her own. When the time is right, they will give you a sign they're ready to meet.

Ask About Your Partner's Wishes

Remember, not all partners will want to be involved with your child. Some might be excited at the opportunity to embrace a new family and become a brilliant stepdad, while others might be nervous or outright refuse to get involved. Before you move forward, discuss how your partner feels, and let them know what you want from them.

It is crucial to align your thinking to be on the same page. If your partner is up for becoming a co-parent and wants to be involved, you can then move on to set boundaries. If they're not, look at how you can create a solution to this, which could be cooling off until they're ready to be more involved. Your children are a permanent fixture in your life, and a partner who refuses to ever invite involvement will likely do nothing but stir up trouble.

Boundaries With Discipline

Self-discipline is one of the trickiest boundaries to negotiate. Every parent has their own set of standards for raising a child, and it's important that your partner knows what those rules are. Otherwise, anarchy is inevitable.

Talk about the bad behavior in your kid that has led to punishment. You might, for instance, limit their TV time to one hour per day; if they throw a fit because they want to watch more, you'd have a system in place to rein them in. The most important thing to remember is that your partner won't automatically know how to behave around your child in these kinds of settings; rather, they will need to be taught.

Also, if your partner has kids, it's important to find out how they discipline them. You need to be on the same page about what kinds of behavior are acceptable and what kinds of behavior are not, as well as the consequences for each. For the sake of your children, you undoubtedly want to cultivate a secure setting for them.

Discuss the degree to which your new partner will help you discipline your child if they do not already have any of their own. Suppose they are ready to discipline while you are not around; always set limits to the sternness they exhibit. If you don't feel at ease with your partner imposing their rigorous set of rules on your child, you should take precautions to prevent this from happening.

What Will You Share About Your Child?

Co-parents frequently need to share a great deal of information about their children, so you should ensure that you are comfortable with this. All relevant parties, including your new partner if they play a significant role in your child's life, should be informed of any transition. If you're worried about forgetting, a collaborative calendar is a great way to keep everyone in the loop and make everyone feel like they're a part of the process.

Should your new partner be included if you and your ex-spouse are already using co-parenting tools? If you want to avoid arguments, talk to your ex before taking any calls.

Keep Communicating With Each Other

Effective communication is the key to learning how to co-parent successfully. Keep in touch with one another as you embark on this journey to discuss what is and isn't working. Make sure your kid is happy with the new dynamic and isn't pining for the old one by keeping up with regular conversations with them.

Conclusion

It's both exciting and nerve-wracking to enter into a new relationship after going through a divorce. After a breakup, not everyone is ready to jump back into the dating pool. Also, few individuals have faith in the durability of new connections.

No matter how many times a relationship doesn't work out, we all still deserve love and passion. Dating after divorce can be interesting, but it's important to keep in mind that no single strategy will work for everyone. Your dating prowess will vary depending on your current situation and emotional state. Dating is an inherently individual experience that calls for patience and emotional maturity.

However, when you are ready to reenter the dating scene following a divorce, there are some guidelines you can follow. Can't wait to find the one? This book might serve as a guide when you're ready to get back into dating.

Consider What You're Searching For

Think about what you want from a partner before you even go on a date. Do you seek a second spouse? Seeking some lighthearted diversion? Do you seek out more committed partnerships? Feelings are likely to shift following a breakup. You may have put an emphasis on serious relationships in the past, but you may be interested in having a summer fling now. This is perfectly normal, but it is important to know what you want before meeting new people.

Value Yourself

Regrettably, many newly single people dive headfirst into the dating pool and strain themselves to match the expectations of prospective suitors. One of the most crucial pieces of advice is to prioritize your own wants and requirements. When dating, it's okay to be self-centered and prioritize your own happiness over that of a potential partner. This will eliminate any potential incompatibilities, leaving you with dates that are willing to work within your parameters.

Contemplate Counseling

Counseling or therapy, even if only for a few sessions, can do wonders for your outlook when you're getting back into the dating scene. Many people now admire their partners for having the emotional intelligence to seek help, and the stigma associated with these services is quickly diminishing. Making the most of your time spent on the first few dates is easier with some expert advice.

Be Honest

Last but not least, always be truthful when dating. It's preferable to start a new relationship with trust and honesty than with lies about the past, even though being vulnerable is daunting. Don't feel bad about your divorce. More appealing than keeping secrets or fibbing is showing that you've moved past your past hurts and are now an emotionally mature adult. If you have preferences, divorcees are more likely to understand your predicament than those who have never been married, so you may want to focus your dating efforts on them.

Whether it's time for you to get back in the game or not, always trust your gut and love yourself before loving someone else. Hopefully, this book has helped you learn more about when to date after a divorce.

Also by the Author

On my way to greatness: Understand the Power of Affirmations, Unlock Your Full Potential and Manifest the Power Within You.

https://www.amazon.com/dp/B0B4R5J935

Highly Productive Teens With MAD Social Skills: thrive with friendship, handle peer pressure, bullying, life challenges and everything in between (The Highly Effective Teens Series).

https://www.amazon.com/dp/B0B8YD6HT1

Highly Productive Teens With MAD Devotional Skills: 52 weeks of encouraging devotions and scriptures, to grow your faith, find hope and inspiration, reclaim your identity, and everything in between (The Highly Effective Teens Series).

https://www.amazon.com/dp/B0BBSN7JGQ

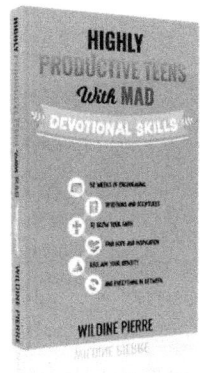

Highly Productive Teens with MAD Life Skills: how to find a job, manage time and money, stay healthy, live independently and everything in between (The Highly Effective Teens Series)

https://www.amazon.com/dp/B0B9HTKCK8

Ladder to Heaven: MOM's Everyday PRAYERS For a Successful SCHOOL YEAR (100 Devotionals+ Scriptures)

https://www.amazon.com/dp/B0BC2FMWK6

References

Bent, J. (2019). *Seven Ways to Keep Your Sanity as You Get Through a Divorce*. Divorce Advice and Coaching for Women | SAS. Retrieved from https://sasforwomen.com/seven-ways-to-keep-your-sanity-as-you-get-through-a-divorce/

Finn, D. K. (2013). *The 8 Keys To Trust In A Post-Divorce Relationship – Part 1*. Dr. Karen Finn. Retrieved from https://drkarenfinn.com/divorce-blog/life-after-divorce/159-the-8-keys-to-trust-in-a-post-divorce-relationship-part-1/

How To Build An Emotional Connection. (n.d.). EverydayHealth.com. Retrieved from https://www.everydayhealth.com/emotional-health/how-build-emotional-connection/

How To Love Yourself Again, After Divorce. (2017). HuffPost. Retrieved from https://www.huffpost.com/entry/how-to-love-yourself-again-after-divorce_b_5930732ae4b042ffa289e87c

How to Navigate Social Media Boundaries in a Relationship. (2017). *The New York Times*. Retrieved from https://www.nytimes.com/2017/08/29/smarter-living/navigating-social-media-relationships.html

Johnson, M. (2019). *Intimacy Isn't Synonymous with Sex*. Healthline. Retrieved from https://www.healthline.com/health/intimacy

KidsNDivorce. (n.d.). *How to Establish Boundaries After Divorce*. PairedLife. Retrieved from https://pairedlife.com/breakups/Establishing-Boundaries-After-Divorce---How-to-Do-It

Learning to Be Happy Again After Your Divorce. (n.d.). Verywell Mind. Retrieved from https://www.verywellmind.com/learning-to-be-happy-again-after-your-divorce-5191473

Mackler, C. (2018). *5 Easy Ways To Communicate Better in Your Relationship*. One Love Foundation. Retrieved from https://www.joinonelove.org/learn/5-easy-ways-to-communicate-better-in-your-relationships/

McElhenney, J. (2022). *Dating Boundaries: How To Establish a Healthy Relationship*. The Whole Parent. Retrieved from https://wholeparentbook.com/dating-boundaries-after-divorce/

No Rules, Just Healthy Boundaries: Talking Relationships. (2021). Psych Central. Retrieved from https://psychcentral.com/blog/why-healthy-relationships-always-have-boundaries-how-to-set-boundaries-in-yours

Palmiotto, J. (2013). *How to Create a Strong Foundation for Your Relationship | Family Guidance & Therapy Center*. Familyguidanceandtherapy.com. Retrieved from https://familyguidanceandtherapy.com/how-to-create-a-strong-foundation-for-your-relationship/

PsyD, A. H. C. (2019). *When Are You Really Ready To Begin Dating After Divorce?* Alicia H. Clark PsyD. Retrieved from https://aliciaclarkpsyd.com/dating-after-divorce/

Setting Healthy Limits–It Can Be an All-Win! - Relationship Problems ?EUR" Tools to Build and Maintain a Healthy Marriage. (n.d.). Retrieved from https://www.mentalhelp.net/blogs/setting-healthy-limits-it-can-be-an-all-win

The New You: Getting to Know (and Love) Yourself Before Dating After Divorce. (n.d.). Divorce Magazine. Retrieved from https://www.divorcemag.com/articles/new-you-getting-to-know-love-yourself-before-dating-after-divorce

5 Key Things to Consider Before You Start Dating After Divorce. (2018). Marriage Advice - Expert Marriage Tips & Advice. Retrieved from https://www.marriage.com/advice/divorce/wait-after-divorce-before-starting-dating-again/

11 Things You Don't Have To Feel Guilty About When Breaking Up With Someone. (n.d.). Bustle. Retrieved from https://www.bustle.com/articles/172229-11-things-you-dont-have-to-feel-guilty-about-when-breaking-up-with-someone

14 Tips for Dating After Divorce. (2019). Oprah Daily. Retrieved from https://www.oprahdaily.com/life/a25858170/tips-for-dating-after-divorce/

Printed in Great Britain
by Amazon